Queering Gay and Lesbian Studies

Queering Gay and Lesbian Studies

THOMAS PIONTEK

UNIVERSITY OF ILLINOIS PRESS
Urbana and Chicago

Library of Congress Cataloging-in-Publication Data

Piontek, Thomas, 1958–
Queering gay and lesbian studies / Thomas Piontek.
p.   cm.
Includes bibliographical references and index.
ISBN-13: 978-0-252-03031-4 (isbn 13 - cloth : alk. paper)
ISBN-10: 0-252-03031-1 (isbn 10 - cloth : alk. paper)
ISBN-13: 978-0-252-07280-2 (isbn 13 - paper : alk. paper)
ISBN-10: 0-252-07280-4 (isbn 10 - paper : alk. paper)
1. Gay and lesbian studies. I. Title.
HQ75.15.P56   2006
306.76'6—dc22   2005012430

For B. B.

Contents

Acknowledgments

For their insightful comments and their encouragement during the conceptual stage of this project, I acknowledge the members of the now-defunct "Crazed Researchers" writing group: Lynda Behan, Anne Bower, Scott Lloyd DeWitt, Marcia Dickson, and Beverly Moss. Throughout the past four years Anne Bower has remained a fiercely loyal friend and an astute and generous critic who offered much love and support, for which I am deeply grateful.

The University of Illinois Press provided engaged and generous reports from two anonymous readers. I thank both of them for the seriousness with which they treated the book prospectus and the initial manuscript. The readers' comments have shaped the final project in important ways. Throughout the entire process, I have greatly appreciated Dr. Willis Regier's enthusiastic support for my project as well as his intelligence and patience. Last but by no means least I thank Bruce Bethell, whose formidable skill as an editor has improved the manuscript considerably.

Several people contributed in a variety of ways to this project, offering friendship, candid criticism, or both. In particular I thank past and present members of the Whitman Circle (Tim Baio, Don Baun, Bob Gordon, Steve Kraynak, Bob Rice, Bud Sawyer, Ken Treadway, and Jack Wisniewski), Andy Aucoin, Henrik Christensen, Howard Fradkin, Patti Lather, Linda Mizejewski, and Doug Zielinki. Finally, throughout these past two years of preparing the manuscript, my partner, Malcolm Cochran, responded to my ever-changing moods with patience, love, and humor. I thank him for understanding my way of looking at the world and letting me get to know and appreciate his.

Parts of chapter 4 first appeared in different form as "Drag Kings und die Performanz des postmodernen Geschlechts," *Testcard: Beiträge zur Popgeschichte* 8 (Mar. 2000): 178–85, and as "Kinging in the Heartland; or, The Power of Marginality," *Journal of Homosexuality* 43, nos. 3–4 (2002): 125–43.

Introduction

In the following pages I attempt to intervene in the conflict between those who see queer theory as the bête noire of gay and lesbian studies and those who embrace it without reservation, believing that "queer studies" should supplant gay and lesbian studies.[1] An explanation of the book's title may help describe the stakes here. On the one hand, queer theory in many ways interrogates gay and lesbian studies, and I thus attempt to elucidate the questions and challenges it has posed to this disciplinary formation. On the other hand, queer theory has *already* "queered" gay and lesbian studies and continues to do so in fundamental ways.

Making gay and lesbian studies perfectly queer is a productive move.[2] At the same time, however, the recent trend to refer to queer-inflected gay and lesbian studies as "queer studies" suggests—prematurely and inaccurately—that queer studies is a mélange, the result of blending two ingredients: gay and lesbian studies and queer theory.[3] To begin with, although the formula "gay and lesbian studies + queer theory = queer studies" seems to suggest an effortless synthesis of the two approaches, the relationship between queer theory and gay and lesbian studies has been anything but simple and harmonious. In fact, the numerous definitions of *queer* that have emerged during the last ten years or so call into question some of the foundations of gay and lesbian studies. The phrase *queer studies* is thus misleading insofar as it misrepresents the merger of queer theory and gay and lesbian studies as a fait accompli. To the contrary, rumors of such a perfect union are greatly exaggerated; consequently, I treat gay and lesbian studies and queer theory as distinct approaches and the relationship between them as a question to be investigated rather than as a fact to be accepted.

Furthermore, I will argue that simply changing gay and lesbian studies to queer studies would risk reducing queer's potential for critical innovation. As critics of queer theory's increased institutionalization have pointed out, "the more it verges on becoming a normative academic discipline, the less queer 'queer theory' can plausibly claim to be," for the queer "gets its critical edge by defining itself against the normal—rather than the heterosexual—and normal includes normal business in the academy."[4] In fact, the queer questions the taken-for-granted assumptions we make about categories and the supposedly stable relations among them, the dichotomies and reifications that characterize a great deal of gay and lesbian work. What I value most about the queer is its potential to challenge the way we make meaning of the world, including the ways in which we think about gender, sexual practice, and identity. Therefore, with a few minor exceptions, I will use the term *queer* to refer not to an identity but to a questioning stance, a cluster of methodologies that lets us explore the taken for granted and the familiar from new vantage points.

If gay and lesbian studies are to thrive in the twenty-first century, it will be vital to queer them, to continue to open gay and lesbian studies to queer critical interventions without further institutionalizing queer theory. Queer theory makes it possible—some might say necessary—to contest beliefs and practices long considered sacrosanct in gay and lesbian studies. In this book I explore in detail the impact that the conflict between the two realms has had in a number of specific fields, from popular culture to politics and history. The categories of "queer" and "gay and lesbian" work differently; each does work the other is ill-equipped or unwilling to do. Consequently, the efficacy of queer versus gay and lesbian ways of thinking and theorizing cannot be determined in general and abstract terms.

In this book I analyze a wide variety of texts—including literature, film, performance, social movements, and radical cultures of sex—and compare queer and gay and lesbian approaches to a variety of questions and problems in order to examine how they function in specific contexts. With a few exceptions, I focus on American cultural phenomena and cultural texts published in the United States. My analyses of texts set or produced elsewhere, moreover, focus on the marketing and reception of these texts in the United States, especially in the context of gay and lesbian studies in the American academy. Of course, as texts such as Cherry Smyth's *Lesbians Talk Queer Notions* and Annamarie Jagose's *Queer Theory: An Introduction* remind us, queer theory has been hotly debated in other English-speaking countries, too, including Great Britain and Australia. Outside the anglophone realm, however, queer theory is frequently treated as an exclusively American phenomenon. I focus on the American situation without assuming that its analysis can or should be applied universally.

Finally, I do not divide this book into a section on queer theory followed by chapters devoted to close readings of literature and other cultural texts. Such an organization would only reinforce the distinction between formalistic literary analysis and cultural critique that enjoins us to think of a literary or cultural text primarily as an aesthetic object apart from the theoretical, social, and political contexts in which it was produced. The cultural texts I analyze in this book both reflect and shape debates in American culture and society about gender, sexual practice, and identity. In fact, I chose them for analysis precisely because of their contribution to these debates, not because of their literary or aesthetic qualities. Consequently, each chapter introduces a theoretical concern that I work through in textual analyses to advance my theoretical argument.

*   *   *

Chapter 1 explores the myth surrounding the 1969 Stonewall Riots, which are generally taken to mark the birth of the contemporary gay and lesbian political movement. In this chapter I analyze how the sign "Stonewall" figures in the demarcation of the gay liberation movement from the homophile movement. In particular, I examine the central role the Stonewall legend has played in creating the notion of "the gay and lesbian community," which implies that all gays and lesbians are in an important sense fundamentally alike. Unfortunately, the concept of a gay identity that supposedly unites people across race, class, gender, and time has resulted in the policing of that identity's boundaries and the concomitant exclusion of the gay community's "others," be they female, nonwhite, working class, or transgendered. This kind of "homonormativity" is exemplified by the misrepresentation of the Stonewall Riots as a rebellion of masculine white men, a characterization that survived unquestioned for decades and has only recently been challenged.

The notion of a coherent and unified gay and lesbian identity also made gays and lesbians candidates for the project of minority history by constituting them as a minority akin to ethnic and racial ones. Minority history lets gays and lesbians be inserted into the historical canon alongside other previously excluded groups. At the same time, however, defining "bad history" as the only problem, and thus merely multiplying the number of historical subjects as a remedy, evades important epistemological questions. Here I take up postmodern challenges to traditional historiography, seeking, among other things, to determine how historical knowledge is produced and how particular viewpoints established dominance and allowed for the exclusion of minority points of view.

In chapter 1 I compare Martin Duberman's historical study *Stonewall* (1993) with Nigel Finch's film adaptation (1995), loosely based on Duberman's book, to illustrate the differences between gay and queer historiography. Duberman's work, I argue, is a representative example of modernist gay history, invested in empiricism and a notion of community predicated on sameness. Finch's film, in contrast, illustrates the postmodern treatment of history, characterized by skepticism about master narratives and the humanist conceptions of identity and subjectivity as unified and stable. Finch's film, in other words, expresses significant doubts concerning our ability to know the past "as it actually was"[5]—a capacity that Duberman's text takes for granted—opting instead for a proliferation of queer fictions of the (gay) past in general and of Stonewall in particular.

In chapter 2 I examine how gay debates about sexuality in the age of AIDS have focused largely on promiscuity, dividing the supposed gay community into two camps, commonly referred to as "sex negatives," who disapprove of promiscuity categorically, and "sex positives," who tend to be staunch defenders of promiscuity. At the same time, the emergence of AIDS prompted people to divide history into two epochs, before and after the disease. This split further characterizes a significant number of literary texts that, since the mid-1980s, have confronted AIDS from a distinctively gay perspective.

To explore and move beyond the problematics of most gay AIDS literature, I consider an early novel by John Champagne, *The Blue Lady's Hands*. Reading Champagne's novel against the backdrop of Foucault's late work on a "practice of the self" allows us to see this work of fiction as providing an alternative to both the before-and-after model of gay history and the monogamy versus promiscuity debate. By introducing a protagonist who strives for his own definitions of love, sex, and homosexual desire outside rigid notions of promiscuity and monogamy, Champagne's novel makes an important contribution to the process of queering the meaning of gay male sexuality in the age of AIDS and can therefore be considered a protoqueer text that helps to reframe the debate over gay sex in gay and lesbian studies.

Exploring the arguments of two generations of sex-positive and sex-negative activists and writers, in this chapter I also investigate why both detractors and defenders of gay promiscuity use rhetoric surprisingly close to that of the religious right when the latter interpret AIDS as punishment for the "sins" of gay liberation. Specifically, I examine the rhetorical conventions that allow for a narration of the past thirty years either as the history of sexual liberation (which sees AIDS as a threat to "post-Stonewall" gains) or as the story of sexual license (which sees AIDS as the logical consequence of gay liberation). My goal in this section is to propose a queer alternative to such binary thinking about gay male sexuality.

In chapter 3 I try to account for a little-noticed yet glaring contradiction in mental-health professionals' attitudes toward homosexuality: the American Psychiatric Association added gender identity disorder (GID) of childhood to its list of mental disorders virtually at the same time it removed homosexuality. This change in medical classification makes it possible to diagnose "gender-dysphoric" children as "protogay" and to advocate early intervention based on the notion that enforcing gender conformity, especially in male children, is the most effective way of preventing adult homosexuality. In this way, homosexuality is redefined as a mental illness, albeit with a different name.

Gay theory and the gay movement were instrumental in the mental-health profession's decision to remove homosexuality from its list of disorders, so why did gay activists not intervene when homosexuality was once again pathologized? In chapter 3 I suggest that one reason for this lack of critical and political intervention may be the fact that both the gay movement and gay theorists were preoccupied with their respective attempts to strip same-sex love of its pathologizing association with gender deviance by demonstrating that gay men are as much "real men" as heterosexual men are. As important as this work has been, it has led to the disavowal of any continuity between the gender-nonconforming child and the gay adult, between the sissy boy and the adult gay man.

In this chapter I analyze representations of gender-deviant childhoods in Richard McCann's short story "My Mother's Clothes: The School of Beauty and Shame" and Alain Berliner's feature film *Ma vie en rose* to explore queer alternatives to the traditional binary conceptualization of gender. These alternatives have the potential to redress the gay movement's betrayal of the sissy boy—no matter what his sexuality eventually turns out to be—by going beyond gay theory's suggested remedy of simply adding homosexual variations to the heterosexual gender matrix.

In chapter 4 I contrast the sometimes violent acts of "gender defenders," who are completely wedded to the notion that there are but two stable, unequivocal genders, with queer challenges to a binary gender system that emphasize the performative aspect of gender. In the beginning of the chapter, I analyze how the drag king phenomenon has been represented in a popular daytime talk show to explore the stakes involved in (mis)reading someone's gender and to analyze the anxieties frequently triggered by nonnormative gender presentations. I consider how and why ambiguous gender can be perceived as a threat to the social order and reveal the thin line between contexts in which gender confusion is the source of titillating entertainment (e.g., the TV talk show) and other situations in which it becomes an excuse for violence—as it did, for example, in the rape and murder of the transsexual Brandon Teena.

In the second half of the chapter I read several performances by a troupe of drag kings in Columbus, Ohio, as exemplifying how queer cultural practices provide alternatives to traditional conceptualizations of feminine versus masculine by exposing the artificiality of conventional gender roles. Finally, I investigate how the playfulness of the drag king act and its anticipation of a world where gender is no longer tied to sexed bodies relate to incidents of gender violence, which constitute a sobering reminder that the pressure to stay within the gender role of one's assigned sex is still frequently a matter of life and death.

In chapter 5 I analyze the widely divergent ways in which gay and lesbian studies and queer theory have approached the issue of nonnormative sexual practices. Queer theory makes sex and sexual practices primary categories for social analysis. This approach departs radically from traditional gay and lesbian studies and mainstream gay politics, which for quite some time have been trying to convince gays and lesbians as well as the straight majority that being gay and lesbian is about more than "just sex." Rather than dismiss "fringe sexualities" as obstacles to the mainstreaming of gays and lesbians, queer theorists have been particularly interested in minority sexual cultures such as S/M and leather sex, not as much for their own sake as for the ways in which these sexual practices complicate our concepts of gender and sexual identity, which are all too often taken for granted in gay and lesbian studies.

In this chapter, by examining autobiographical, ethnographic, and literary accounts of sexual-minority communities, I articulate the creative and transformative potential of queer sex. I pay particular attention to the ways in which the theater of S/M challenges the traditional organization of desire along lines of gender and sexual identity and the ways in which nongenital forms of pleasure (such as fisting) multiply the body's "erogenous zones." By questioning the ways in which bodies are culturally mapped, sexual subcultures such as these are able to suspend boundaries of gender and sexual orientation in their sex play—categories that have been foundational in defining gay and lesbian studies.

1

Forget Stonewall: Making Gay History
Perfectly Queer

We are the Stonewall girls
We wear our hair in curls
We wear no underwear
We show our pubic hair
We wear our dungarees
Above our nelly knees!

—a chorus line of mocking queens
confronting the police outside
the Stonewall Inn

WE HOMOSEXUALS PLEAD WITH OUR PEOPLE TO PLEASE
HELP MAINTAIN PEACEFUL AND QUIET CONDUCT
ON THE STREETS OF THE VILLAGE—MATTACHINE

—a sign on the boarded-up façade of
the Stonewall Inn

The 1970s and subsequent decades have spawned a proliferation of writing frequently described as "minority history," a term that encompasses various subordinate groups' struggles to recover histories previously overlooked or excluded. Minority history has met with considerable resistance from consensus historians, who claim that the political use of history jeopardizes the historian's scholarly integrity.[1] John Boswell, a Yale professor who wrote perhaps the most popular work of gay history, *Christianity, Social Tolerance, and Homosexuality*, addresses these anxieties about a politicization of the historical profession in a 1989 essay:

Since the exclusion of minorities from much historiography prior to the twentieth century was related to or caused by concerns other than purely scholarly interest, their inclusion now, even for purely political ends, not only ends a previous "political" distortion, but provides a more complete data base for judgments about the historical issues involved. Such truth as is yielded by historical analysis generally emerges from the broadest possible synthesis of the greatest number of viewpoints and vantages: the addition of minority history and viewpoints to twentieth-century historiography is a net gain for all concerned.[2]

Although clearly intended as an impassioned defense of "minority history," Boswell's argument raises a number of issues, including the conceptual differences between a modernist gay history and a postmodernist queer history.[3] For one thing, Boswell considers the "problem" of minority history exclusively in terms of traditional definitions of history. Bracketing issues of power, he represents history as a pluralistic enterprise aiming for the greatest possible combination of viewpoints. But replacing an oppressive consensus with a liberating synthesis provides little in the way of a conceptual transformation.[4] Does not a new synthesis risk producing yet another historical master narrative that reduces difference precisely by accommodating it? Thus, when Boswell claims that adding hitherto silenced stories has been a boon for history, he is ignoring conflicts over the way historical knowledge is produced and the struggle for hegemony that has characterized debates within the discipline.[5] Boswell's rhetoric thus suggests that, provided everybody is allowed on board, there's no need to rock the boat.

From a queer perspective, however, the project of gay history involves more than simply adding information. As I pointed out in the introduction, the queer defines itself against multiple regimes of the normal, and I agree with Scott Bravmann that we should look at history as one such regime.[6] Consequently, reclaiming the gay and lesbian past can never mean simply inserting previously excluded groups into the historical canon. Such a strategy permits at best purely cosmetic changes, not structural ones, for it portrays the problem solely as being bad history instead of questioning the way history has been traditionally constructed. At the same time, the multiplication of subjects and stories also raises epistemological questions. For example, Joan W. Scott argues that the "proliferation of Others' histories [. . .] has exposed the politics by which one particular viewpoint established predominance."[7] Therefore, instead of merely developing another master narrative—one that can synthesize "minority" viewpoints without being fundamentally altered by them—we need to examine the modes of knowledge seeking that have made history an exclusionary practice in the first place.

Furthermore, the term *minority* seems problematic when applied to gay men and lesbians, for it raises exactly the kinds of questions that have polarized debates between gay and lesbian studies and queer theory: Can sexual orientation constitute a minority? If so, under what conditions? How does a minority thus constituted compare to ethnic and racial minorities? Is such a minoritizing view of lesbians and gay men politically advantageous, or does it restrict possibilities of political intervention? These questions are crucial to any consideration of gay history, and their discussion should not be foreclosed by a terminology that falsely suggests them to have already been answered. The constraints of modernist historical narratives are compounded when gay history relies on modernist notions of a "gay identity" uniting people across divides of race, sex, class, and time.

Analyzing the history of attitudes toward homosexuality in the Christian West, Boswell's *Christianity, Social Tolerance, and Homosexuality,* for example, argues that a gay identity and gay people can be found throughout history. A queer approach to history writing, however, refuses the notion of a total history, casts doubts on attempts to write gay history in conventional historical styles, reconceives historical representation, and ultimately seeks to reframe the very meaning of history itself. Perhaps nothing illustrates the differences between the two approaches better than does a comparison between gay history's interpretation of Stonewall as a "unifying and originary historical moment from which the present logically and coherently follows"[8] and a queer reading of Stonewall as showing the impossibility of offering a singular interpretation of any particular event.

Before Stonewall

On the dust jacket of the historian Martin Duberman's best-selling book *Stonewall* (1993), the Stonewall Riots, today generally taken to mark the birth of the "modern" gay and lesbian political movement,[9] are described as follows: "The Stonewall Inn was a gay bar in New York's Greenwich Village. At a little after one A.M. on the morning of June 28, 1969, the police carried out a routine raid on the bar. But it turned out not to be routine at all. Instead of cowering—the usual reaction to a police raid—the patrons inside Stonewall and the crowd that gathered outside the bar fought back against the police. The five days of rioting that followed changed forever the face of lesbian and gay life." For more than three decades the riots have been memorialized with commemorative celebrations in the month of June throughout this country and around the world. Indeed, Duberman claims, "'Stonewall' is *the* emblematic event in modern lesbian and gay history."[10] Yet Duberman, along with many others, is critical of this attribution of meaning to the historical event. He argues that "we have, since 1969, been trading the same few tales about the Riots from the same few accounts—trading them for so long that they have transmogrified into simplistic myth."[11]

In *Beginnings* Edward Said examines the obsession with his book's epony-mous topic, which he claims has occupied thought since the eighteenth cen-tury. Beginnings, according to Said, function as "intervening techniques that deliver reality to us in palpable form." He adds that they allow us to "create sequences, periods, forms, and measurements that suit our perceptual needs. Once we have seen them, these orders are left alone: we assume that they go on ordering to time's end, and there is nothing we can do about it. These mediating orders are in turn commanded and informed by one or another moderately intelligible force, whether we call it history, time, mind, or [. . .] language."[12] Because historical events (and memories of them) imbue the present with meaning, one of the most instructive questions to explore is how the emphasis on Stonewall as a beginning has influenced the way we understand gay history before and after 1969.

One possible answer emerges from the way this question has been phrased: the focus on Stonewall as a beginning constitutes this event as a watershed and thus suggests a qualitative difference between the times on the two sides of the divide—before and after Stonewall. Thus, the mythology that has de-veloped around Stonewall posits a radical difference between developments during the past thirty-five years and anything that happened before "those heady, sweltering nights in June 1969."[13] This perception, however, is merely the result of the plotting (or emplotment) of history around a specific, sup-posedly pivotal event, which inevitably risks creating a misleading before-and-after historiography through its overemphasis on discontinuity.[14]

The insistence on the Stonewall Riots as a point of rupture, a radical break with the past, fabricates a historical scheme in which Stonewall sepa-rates the past repression of gay culture from its present glorious realization: once upon a time, there was no gay organizing/movement/community; then came Stonewall, and now there is gay organizing/movement/community. The past becomes an amorphous mass without any distinguishing features, a block of time reaching, as it were, all the way from Stonehenge to Stonewall, during which there was only unrelieved oppression. In contrast, Stonewall itself is represented as an *absolute* beginning, the zero degree of gay and lesbian liberation. In fact, Stonewall has been called a watershed event so often that it would be impossible to list all the occurrences. One particularly extreme example of such a formulation comes from the lesbian separatist Jill Johnston. In her introduction to McDarrah and McDarrah's *Gay Pride:*

Photographs from Stonewall to Today, Johnston writes: "I think of Stonewall myself as an event dividing time into B.C. (before consciousness) and A.D. (after death—of the life before consciousness)."[15] Moving along similar lines, cultural critics such as Michael Denneny and David Bergman have described the post-Stonewall 1970s as a golden decade characterized by social transformation, increased freedom, and the burgeoning productivity of gay writers and artists.[16]

Reacting to this formulation, a number of gay and lesbian historians have questioned celebrating Stonewall as a beginning. Eric Marcus, for example, argues that "this misconception [of Stonewall as the origin of the gay and lesbian movement] has been reflexively asserted [. . .] so often and for so many years that it would seem to be an unassailable fact."[17] The director Greta Schiller makes a similar point in her award-winning documentary film *Before Stonewall* (1986), which combines oral history interviews with newsreels, clips from Hollywood movies, television news broadcasts, photographs, and personal memorabilia belonging to individual gay men and lesbians. As Schiller and her research director, Andrea Weiss, explain in their guide to the film, the juxtaposition of these seemingly disparate materials allowed them to challenge "the historical invisibility of gay people" even in contexts where, because of culturally conditioned ways of seeing, "we are so used to not seeing homosexuality."[18] The result is a chronicle of gay and lesbian communities from about the turn of the century to the late 1960s—a history from a time supposedly before there was any history.

The historian John D'Emilio takes on this misconception about Stonewall as well. He argues that "mass movements for social change do not spring full-blown into existence, like Athena from the forehead of Zeus. Movements have roots; they have origins. Surely [. . .] *something* of significance must have occurred before that night of outrage in Greenwich Village to explain why a spontaneous riot could have birthed a mass grass-roots movement."[19] Furthermore, the celebration of Stonewall as the birth of the gay and lesbian movement seems puzzling, for birth primarily signifies progression from one generation to the next, so that the metaphor ultimately implies exactly the kind of continuity that the insistence on a radically new beginning belies.[20]

D'Emilio's groundbreaking *Sexual Politics, Sexual Communities: The Making of A Homosexual Minority in the United States, 1940–1970* demonstrates that the political efforts of gay men and lesbians in the 1970s were preceded by a generation of men and women in the 1950s and 1960s who composed the "homophile" movement, comprising such organizations as the Mattachine Society and the Daughters of Bilitis. D'Emilio concludes that many of the shifts that occurred in the 1970s "were due to the weakening of traditional centers of powers caused by the protest movements of the 1960s, but the relative ease with which gay liberationists accumulated victories can only be explained by the persistent, plodding work of the activists who preceded them. The homophile movement deserves kinder treatment than it has received. The popular wisdom of gay liberation needs to be reevaluated."[21] The misreading of Stonewall yields two important questions that lie beyond D'Emilio's suggested remedy of a "kinder" historical treatment of the homophile movement: First, why did gay activists in the 1970s claim Stonewall as the beginning of their movement even as they were working alongside people from various homophile organizations? Second, why has the creation myth surrounding Stonewall been so durable?[22]

Why Stonewall?

Duberman, Marcus, D'Emilio, and Schiller have successfully challenged the notion that Stonewall initiated the modern gay and lesbian movement by providing ample evidence of gay and lesbian organizing and community building in previous decades. Surprisingly, however, only Marcus attempts to divest Stonewall of its singular status. He argues that by investing so much in Stonewall, we not only diminish all that came before but also tie everything that has happened since to this mythic event. Stonewall, according to Marcus, should be considered one significant moment in the history of the gay and lesbian movement rather than its single point of origin. Significantly, this shift is also implied by the historical period Marcus examines in his book, the forty-five years from 1945 to 1990. He denies Stonewall any of the special attention usually lavished on events believed to mark either the beginning or the end of an era.

In contrast to Marcus's approach—and despite their stated desire to challenge the origin myth surrounding Stonewall—Duberman's and D'Emilio's books, as well as Schiller's documentary, leave intact and even help to perpetuate the event's status as a watershed. Both D'Emilio and Duberman end their respective studies with the formation of the Gay Liberation Front (GLF), which they represent as a direct result of the events at the Stonewall Inn. Schiller's film is framed by the very myth it seeks to debunk, beginning and ending as it does with footage of the Stonewall Riots. Thus the structure of these three texts, wittingly or not, maintains Stonewall as the critical break with the past, suggesting that Stonewall did in fact inaugurate a history different in kind from the one that they set out to tell. Despite their creators' intentions—to challenge the creation myth surrounding Stonewall—these texts end up suggesting that the course of gay and lesbian history *did* change overnight in June 1969, that gay liberation was born at the Stonewall Inn. In a paradoxical way, D'Emilio, Duberman, and Schiller thus confirm the singular status of Stonewall as the beginning of one era precisely by representing it as the end of another.

A chapter entitled "A New Beginning: The Birth of Gay Liberation" further documents how D'Emilio undercuts his own stated desire to open up the history of gay and lesbian liberation. In this chapter he discusses a hastily assembled special edition of the New York Mattachine Society's newsletter characterizing the events at the Stonewall Inn with the headline "The Hairpin Drop Heard Round the World." He comments: "Before the end of July, women and men in New York had formed the Gay Liberation Front. [. . .] Word of the Stonewall Riots and GLF spread rapidly among the networks of young radicals scattered across the country, and within a year gay liberation groups had sprung into existence on college campuses and in cities around the nation."[23] D'Emilio's assessment culminates in the assertion that the Stonewall Riots sparked a "nationwide grassroots 'liberation' effort among gay men and women,"[24] a claim that cannot be sustained by the kind of empirical evidence historians such as D'Emilio himself and Duberman offer. Perhaps the question is not so much whether Stonewall was a beginning but whether it could have been *perceived* as a beginning at the time.

A comparison between the Stonewall Riots and another kind of mythic moment in American history, the assassination of John F. Kennedy, can shed some light on this question and usefully queer the notion of beginnings. Most gay men and lesbians would no doubt be hard-pressed to come up with an answer if asked where they were during the riots. Of course, Stonewall and the Kennedy assassination are events of a different order; my focus, however, is on their mythological constructions. Thus, perhaps Stonewall was severely underreported precisely because, unlike Kennedy's assassination, it was not immediately discernible as a "historical moment." Duberman, for example, points out that many affluent gay men who spent the weekend at Fire Island or in the Hamptons either caught up with the news belatedly or heard about the rioting and ignored it. According to her own account, Sylvia Rivera, one of the people Duberman interviewed for his book, was at the Stonewall Inn on the first night of the riots, yet even she heard nothing about the sudden emergence of the GLF and joined its successor organization, the Gay Activists Alliance (GAA), only in February 1970. Rivera, Duberman explains, was "cut off from her usual contacts" as a result of living and working in New Jersey.[25]

These two passages from Duberman's history certainly undermine the assertion that the news of Stonewall and the formation of the GLF in New York City spread like wildfire all across the nation, as D'Emilio and others have claimed. If news about the riots did not travel across the Hudson River or along Long Island Sound, why would we assume that it traveled the much farther distance to gay men and lesbians in the Midwest and the South or on the West Coast? Perhaps D'Emilio's reference to widespread networks of young radicals provides an important clue. He seems to imply a distinction between radical gay activists organized in networks and the gay and lesbian population at large. This division in turn implies that the gay and lesbian community these activists were supposedly representing and fighting for was still under construction—and the mythology of Stonewall was to play a crucial part in that construction.

Unlike the Kennedy assassination, which at least in popular culture is frequently considered to mark the end of an era, Stonewall traditionally has been deemed to mark the beginning of a new age. Importantly, whereas the sense of an ending can be experienced concurrently with the event that marks it, the designation of a beginning is often made after the fact, after the event that is subsequently constituted as a beginning. This distinction is significant, for, as Said argues, one rarely searches for prior beginnings "unless the present matters a great deal": "It is my present urgency, the here and now, that will enable me to establish the sequence of beginning-middle-end and to transform it from a distant object—located 'there'—into the subject of my reasoning. So conceived and fashioned, time and space yield a sequence authorized by a wish for [. . .] significance."[26] It is important to note that the search for beginnings, or rather one particular beginning, manifests an intentionality that in turn governs the search: "one beginning is permissible; another one like it, at a different time or place, is not permissible."[27] A beginning assumes a privileged position in the process of (re-)reading the past: "a beginning *authorizes:* it constitutes an authorization for what follows from it."[28] Therefore, despite what logic or common sense might lead us to believe, beginnings do not determine what follows. On the contrary, in what appears to be a paradox of historiography, the choice of a beginning is preceded by the declaration of an intention. In other words, without an intention there will be no beginning.

Perhaps this rather abstract notion can best be explained with the help of an example. In his introduction to a collection of essays about gay liberation,

D'Emilio relates how he first heard about the events at the Stonewall Inn. He and his lover were touring Europe during the summer of 1969, and one August day in Paris he picked up a copy of the *Village Voice* that described the riots. He comments: "We knew this was important, but also didn't quite know what to make of it."[29] D'Emilio does not explain how he knew this news story was important; perhaps he intuited that the events might be raw material for the writing of history. What is relevant here, however, is the inconsistency of D'Emilio's recollection, which assigns general importance without assigning a specific meaning. What I suggest is that the specific significance of the riots remained unclear to D'Emilio precisely because the event had not yet been "authorized" as a beginning. What is at stake, then, is the difference between an event—the Stonewall Riots—and the framing of that event as the beginning of a continuous sequence—the history of gay liberation. It is this posteriority that D'Emilio lacked when he read about the riots in the summer of 1969. This lack of a posterior perspective in turn prevented him from grasping what would eventually emerge as the mythological significance of Stonewall. Ultimately, the authorization of a beginning amounts to nothing less than the crucial first step in the process of rereading the past in the light of a retrospectively articulated telos.

The fact that we can draw meaning from Stonewall only in the context of the belatedly constructed teleology of gay liberation is further illustrated by a passage from Allen Young's 1971 essay "Out of the Closets, into the Streets." The first paragraph of his article renders a familiar tale in a familiar way: "On a June evening in 1969 police began what seemed like a routine raid on the Stonewall Inn, Greenwich Village's most popular gay men's bar. But the raid didn't go off as planned. We fought back. The gay liberation movement was born." The first sentence of the next paragraph, however, calls attention both to the frailty of memory and its mythmaking character: "I am smiling ironically as I write 'we.' I wasn't there, and it took me more than six months before I even began to take part in the gay liberation movement."[30] Although in the first paragraph Young identifies himself (retrospectively) as having participated in the birth of gay liberation, he in fact missed the happy occasion—not only because he was not present at the Stonewall Inn that particular night but, more important, because he became aware of the riots and the myth that had been created around them only after gay liberation was already experiencing its first teething troubles.

Gay radicals designated Stonewall as the inaugural event of gay liberation to achieve their specific goals, but this becomes clear only when we question the standard before-and-after, us-and-them dichotomy constructed around

Stonewall, using a queer perspective to reveal the overlapping attitudes and forms of activism that existed in the past. For gay radicals, Stonewall functioned as an enabling instrument in their conflict with the homophile movement, and the metaphorical connotations of the bar's name and its compound parts—stone and wall—helped to make it a sign for an event of resistance. No poet or novelist could have intentionally devised a name more expressive of the characteristics of the "new" gay liberation movement. The name connotes toughness, solidity, resistance, and steadfastness. A stone wall is also a line of demarcation, separating two spaces absolutely from each other—one side and the other or, metaphorically speaking, the before and the after. Would Stonewall have been so easily mythologized if the bar had been named something else?

The rhetorical rather than empirical basis for choosing Stonewall as the beginning of the gay movement is further illustrated by Kayla Jay and Allen Young, who recall that in the wake of Stonewall, New York City's GLF was formed mainly by two elements: "One was composed of members of the old homophile organizations, such as the Mattachine Society of New York and the Daughters of Bilitis, who had been fighting for acceptance since the 1950s. Another, younger group consisted of people like us who had experience with the New Left, the counterculture, the civil rights movement, or feminism."[31] This passage raises an important question: considering that this and other accounts portray homophile organizers and gay activists, despite their differences, as working side by side in organizations such as the Gay Liberation Front, how was it possible to forget about the contributions of the homophile movement? Perhaps the more revealing question, however, is why it was (or at least appeared to be) necessary to repress any memory of the homophile movement's contributions. The rhetoric of the passage suggests that by juxtaposing the "old homophile organizations" and the "younger group" of gay radicals, Jay and Young represent the discord between the two groups in terms of a generational conflict—a rhetorical move that recalls the 1960s maxim "Don't trust anyone over thirty." Furthermore, this characterization suggests that, to claim an identity of their own, they had to figuratively "kill the father" by openly challenging the authority of the older generation.[32]

In the context of this generational conflict, the younger generation is associated with a certain militancy, while the older activists are frequently disqualified as assimilationist. Not at all coincidentally, the gay militants chose the name Gay Liberation Front in homage to the Vietnamese guerrillas and their National Liberation Front. The name, however, also refers to a marked difference between gay radicals and their predecessors. Gay liberationists considered themselves a component of the decade's radical movement for social change, part of a front in the political sense of the word (a collection of groups). They saw gay oppression as one social issue among many and also opposed capitalism, racism, sexism, and the Vietnam War. In the words of Allen Young, writing in 1971, "gay liberation is a total revolutionary movement."[33] Along similar lines, the sign "Stonewall" was in the beginning essentially tied to the sign "riots." By semiotic correspondence, the sign "Stonewall Riots" ties the gay and lesbian movement to the Watts Riots; to the student uprisings at Kent and Jackson State (among others); and perhaps most crucially, to the previous summer's riots at the Democratic Convention in Chicago. This correspondence of riots figures Stonewall as normative, part of a larger movement for peace and (sexual) liberation.

The militant gays' attempt to place gay liberation in the context of a larger movement for social change may also be one reason they felt it necessary to denigrate the achievements of the homophile movement and to pass over the older generation in silence. Perhaps, D'Emilio suggests, gay liberationists denied the importance of their forebears because homophile organizations such as the Mattachine Society "had a reputation as the 'NAACP of our movement,' a damning description during years when groups like the Black Panther party were capturing the fancy of young radicals."[34] For gay militants committed to a utopian vision encapsulated by the slogan "revolution in our lifetime," affirming their own radicalism inevitably meant proclaiming their radical dissimilarity from those who came before them.

To be sure, the homophile movement as it existed in 1969 was anything but radical. The Mattachine Society in particular was uncomfortable with any nonconforming behavior other than homosexuality. As Duberman argues, its members were "primarily interested in winning acceptance on the mainstream's own terms, not in challenging mainstream values; they regarded themselves as patriots and good Americans; and they preferred to rely on 'experts' rather than on political organizing to plead their cause—having internalized the view of that era's prime experts, the psychiatrists, that their 'condition' was pathological."[35] The dominant message to other gays was to "straighten up" and project an image that would not shock middle-class sensibilities, thus achieving tolerance from heterosexual society. Such an approach surely deserves to be called conservative and assimilationist.

This, however, is only part of the story. Things were decidedly different in 1950, when the Mattachine Society was founded by five men in Los Angeles, among them the activist Harry Hay. The men had been members of the

Communist Party, a fact reflected not only in their tactics but also in their early radicalism. The group had a cell structure, and new members were recruited through discussions sponsored by the Mattachine Foundation, the organization's public face. One of the society's first activities was to defend its member Dale Jennings, who had been arrested for soliciting while out cruising. His subsequent acquittal was the first for an openly gay man charged with lewd vagrancy. Duberman describes the group's development as follows:

> The Mattachine analysis of homosexuality was, at its inception, startlingly radical. This small group of some dozen men pioneered the notion—which from mid-1953 to 1969 fell out of favor in homophile circles, only to be picked up by gay activists after 1969—that gays were a legitimate minority within a hostile mainstream culture. They further argued that most gays had internalized the society's negative judgment of them as "sick," that such "false consciousness" had to be challenged, and that political struggle was the best vehicle for doing so.[36]

As this passage implies, the society's direction changed drastically in 1953. A convention in Los Angeles marked its takeover by a more assimilationist strand of gay thinking and the end of many of the original founders' involvement. In fact, the new leaders threatened to give the FBI the names of any members who were also members of the Communist Party unless they resigned. It has to be pointed out, however, that the conservative reign of the Mattachine Society, and the homophile movement in general, did not go unchallenged from mid-1953 to 1969, as the passage from D'Emilio's history may falsely suggest. Barbara Gittings, cofounder of the Daughters of Bilitis, argues that significant "consciousness changes were definitely fomenting in the sixties, well before Stonewall."[37] One of these changes involved the growing criticism of kowtowing to medical experts, psychiatrists in particular. Therefore, Gittings maintains, Stonewall "doesn't represent a distinctly changed consciousness in the movement. The militancy—the 'we are the experts, not these non-Gays'—all that developed well before Stonewall, thanks largely to Frank Kameny; he was the first one who articulated a complete, coherent philosophy for the Gay movement."[38] Influenced by the civil rights movement and its more aggressive direct-action tactics, Kameny criticized the homophile movement's respect for professionals and rejected medical theories about the causes of homosexuality. Speaking to the New York Mattachine Society in 1964, he argued:

I do not see the NAACP and CORE worrying about which chromosome and gene produced a black skin, or about the possibility of bleaching the Negro. . . . I do not see any great interest on the part of the B'nai B'rith Anti-Defamation League in the possibility of solving problems of anti-semitism by converting Jews to Christians. . . . We are interested in obtaining rights for our respective minorities AS Negroes, AS Jews, and AS HOMOSEXUALS. Why we are Negroes, Jews, or Homosexuals is totally irrelevant, and whether we can be changed to Whites, Christians, or heterosexuals is equally irrelevant.[39]

Along with Kameny, many gay men and lesbians who were invested in the civil rights struggle challenged the neutrality espoused by the homophile movement during the 1960s. While conservatives managed to keep the upper hand, the divisions in the movement became more and more pronounced. The picture that emerges from these and other accounts calls into question the simplistic distinction between an assimilationist pre-Stonewall era and the gay radicalism of the 1970s.

The "Stonewall generation," then, pioneered neither the radical stance of the gay movement nor its militant tactics. In fact, gay militants in the early 1970s picked up where the founders of Mattachine had left off in the early 1950s, continuing a tradition of radical gay politics established by the early homophile movement. The claim that the gay movement constituted a radical break with homophile politics should be understood as a function of the revolutionary rhetoric and historiographic conceptualization that gay radicals required. As Said argues, "to have begun means to be the first to have done something, the first to have initiated a course discontinuous with other courses. What is first, because it is first, because it *begins*, is eminent. Most utopian models derive their force from this logic. The beginning as first point in a given continuity has exemplary strength equally in history, in politics, and in intellectual discipline—and perhaps each of these domains preserves the myth of a beginning utopia of some kind as a sign of its distinct identity."[40]

Significantly, the question of identity to which Said refers links individual and societal innovation—changing minds as well as material conditions. This connection is a crucial one when discussing gay liberation in general and Stonewall in particular. In addition, this link helps us understand why gay liberationists employed Stonewall in their attempts to advance their political agenda. Capitalizing on "the implausible fact that, for once, cops, not gays, had been routed,"[41] they transformed what one reporter pejoratively termed the "forces of faggotry"[42] into *gay power,* a force to be reckoned with. Stonewall literally and figuratively marked the moment when "limp wrists were forgotten."[43] As D'Emilio contends, "The new generation of gay liberationists saved the Stonewall Riots from being simply 'an event.' They fleshed out the implications of the Riots, and ensured that they would become the symbol of a new militancy."[44] Stonewall, in other words, became an enabling fiction that allowed gay militants to read back into history a particular story they wanted to tell—the story of gay liberation as they envisioned it.

Who Owns Stonewall?

Again, members of the Gay Liberation Front sought to prove their radicalism by denying any continuity between their organization and the homophile movement, disavowing the latter's radical beginning. These measures were part of what Duberman calls an attempt by a "newly assertive generation [. . .] to establish its own hegemony."[45] It is therefore somewhat ironic that radicalism suffered a fate similar to that of the homophile movement, soon losing its status as the dominant tendency of the post-Stonewall movement. Almost from its inception, the Gay Liberation Front was the subject of some-times severe criticism. Only six months after the riots, on 21 December 1969, nineteen people meeting in a Greenwich Village apartment created a platform for those who disagreed with the GLF's philosophy and tactics by constitut-ing a new organization, the Gay Activists Alliance (GAA). Whereas the GLF considered the fate of gay people in the context of a broader revolutionary movement, the GAA was exclusively dedicated to securing basic rights for homosexuals by working within the system.

But the formation of the GAA did not spell the immediate demise of the GLF; in fact, the two organizations coexisted for a few years. In retrospect, Jay and Young consider these early developments as an indication of the things that were to come in the following twenty-five years: "The Gay Activists Al-liance [. . .] and later more professional and organized efforts[,] such as the National Gay Task Force (later renamed the National Gay and Lesbian Task Force and still in existence), soon took gay liberation down another path. The goals of 'gay rights'—assuming a place for us in existing society rather than pursuing a utopian vision—began to replace 'gay revolution.'"[46]

Like Jay and Young, many were frustrated by the shift from revolution back to reform and from a broadly defined political struggle to single-issue politics. Gay liberationists had been confident that one of the basic tenets of their movement, coming out, would create an army of permanent recruits. As D'Emilio argues, in the 1950s and 1960s the "enticements of the closet" had been "far more alluring than anything activists could offer." Gay activists in the aftermath of Stonewall, however, successfully challenged the "regime of the closet."[47] Coming out became the quintessential expression of 1960s radicalism and the fusion of the personal and the political that it exalted.

As gay and lesbian liberationists came out of the closet, their example proved infectious to many other men and women who were not embedded in the radical politics of the 1960s. For many of these new recruits, equitable acceptance into the mainstream of American society replaced revolution as a political goal.[48] The trend toward a one-issue, identity-based reform politics was further increased by the concept of "sexual orientation," which gained currency during the late 1970s and 1980s. The appeal to sexual orientation made it possible to conceive of gay and lesbians as a social minority group akin to ethnic minorities demanding civil rights.

Gay rights activists, like the homophiles they have often disparaged, are characterized by a highly pronounced respect for the middle-class sensibilities of mainstream America. Randy Wicker, a pioneer activist and member of the Mattachine Society who subscribed to the idea that gays are just like straights except for their sexual orientation, spoke for many homophiles in criticizing the spectacle of the Stonewall Riots: "Screaming queens forming chorus lines and kicking went against everything that I wanted people to think about homosexuals [for it suggested] that we were a bunch of drag queens in the Village acting disorderly and tacky and cheap."[49] While the tone of that statement may seem ludicrous today—does forming a chorus line really qualify as disorderly conduct?—the sentiments Wicker expresses are still very much with us.

In the 1980s and 1990s the "success" of the gay movement continued to include some of the same attitudes Wicker had expressed. Admittedly, the high number of elected and appointed officials from the local to the federal level (including David Mixner, adviser to President Clinton and the first openly gay senior White House aide) marked enormous progress for the gay movement. Nonetheless, this success continued to be turned against "the gay community" by its very representatives, dividing various gay and lesbian constituencies against one another by attempting to enforce a party line that, just like the notion of "respectability" itself, was middle class, white, and primarily male. The same sense of class propriety that Wicker saw violated at the Stonewall Riots governed mainstream gay politics in the 1990s. Thus, the openly gay congressman Barney Frank, speaking at a forum for gay civil rights at the National Press Club, maintained that the gay community should emphasize mainstream themes to win broad political support. According to

Frank, self-expression may be healthy, but it does not translate into an effective political movement: "The Gay rights movement shouldn't stress the most extreme aspects of Gay culture if it wants to gain political support and strength."[50] The extremes against which Frank cautions are perpetrated by those whom he calls the "fringe elements" of the community, people who (in his eyes) indulge in wanton displays of their gender or sexual identities. Such behavior, he argues, undermines the cause.

What are the most "extreme" aspects of gay culture and which people constitute the "fringe elements" of the gay community? The gay media's coverage of gay pride parades provides an unequivocal answer to these questions. Every year the gay press devotes the weeks before Gay Pride Week to a well-rehearsed discussion of whether leathermen and drag queens should be allowed to participate in parades representing "the gay community." While the Dykes on Bikes are a popular mainstay of San Francisco's annual Gay Pride Parade, the participation of "cross-dressed" lesbians on motorcycles remains contested in some midwestern cities. (Similar consternation emerged over a contingent of bare-chested lesbians in the 1993 March on Washington and the 1999 Gay Pride Rally in Columbus, Ohio.)

Paradoxically, although today's gay movement traces its origins to the radicalism of the Stonewall generation, what seems to have endured is a peculiar sense of respectability that clearly predates Stonewall. Commenting on the gay community's renunciation of transvestites, Sylvia Rivera, a drag queen who participated in the Stonewall Riots, explains, "I hurt for the simple fact that the movement never recognized the drag queen until this year [1989], twenty years after Stonewall. It was always, 'We must wear a suit and tie. We have to look part of their world. We can't be different.'"[51] Of course, there is more at stake than a dispute over fashion. Wearing a suit and tie, in Rivera's book of rules, would be tantamount to passing for straight, which simply has never been an option for her: "I couldn't have passed, not in this lifetime."[52]

More important, Rivera's lament highlights an erroneous assumption underlying the assertion of a coherent collective gay and lesbian identity—namely, that all those involved in same-sex relations, whether lesbians or gay men, are fundamentally alike. The consolidation of a unified gay and lesbian identity in turn requires the exclusion of difference and the policing of that identity's boundaries. Tony Coron, who considers himself a political conservative, puts it this way: "Going to a gay pride parade every year becomes a personal challenge. I have a little trouble with the weirdness—the leathermen and drag floats."[53]

This concern about respectability and an utter irreverence for traditional categories of gender and sexuality were both present at Stonewall. They were symbolized, for example, by the sign the Mattachine Society put on the boarded-up façade of the Stonewall Inn and the line of mocking drag queens kicking up their heels in front of the bar, both quoted as epigraphs to this chapter. Ultimately, however—after some historiographical work—the myth of Stonewall came to mean that gay men and lesbians had joined the mainstream, albeit to the left of center.

Under the sign "Stonewall" gay and lesbian activists joined a larger movement for social change—the Movement, to use the name favored by those in it—and so found a legitimacy that they had not had before. Originally conceived as a catalyst for a radical political change, Stonewall eventually became the central trope of a mainstream gay culture that grounded its conceptions of gay identity within "the specific experiences of urban, middle-class white men."[54] This transformation of Stonewall no doubt helped lead to the hegemony of rights-oriented gay activists, for whom liberation means simply extending the legacy of American freedoms to homosexuals in a pluralistic society. Today, however, queer activists echo gay radicals from the early 1970s in arguing that mainstream American society is built essentially on the principle of the exclusion of homosexuals, women, and people of color. This contradiction suggests that, in the process of making themselves a potent political and social force, gay men and lesbians have elided some of the more uncomfortable questions in favor of the powerful and empowering mythology of Stonewall. Perhaps the challenge today is once again to recognize Stonewall as a messy and ambiguous historical event that allows us to account for the ways in which the experience of homosexuality is inflected by multiple differences that are obscured by the modernist insistence on a homogeneous homosexual identity. Multiplying the meaning of Stonewall may help us to acknowledge differences among queer people, including differences of race, gender, and class, as well as different approaches to the project of gay and lesbian liberation. As it stands, Stonewall reminds us that, while we may have come out, we still have a few skeletons in the closet.

Who Was at Stonewall—and Why It Matters

In the decade following the riots, Stonewall was represented as a rebellion of white men. Only in the mid-1980s did gay historians begin to challenge the traditional representation of the events as an all-male, all-white revolt. According to more recent accounts, from Duberman's book to an *Advocate* cover story entitled "Stonewall's Eyewitnesses," gay men *and* lesbians fought back in 1969; moreover, many of them were people of color, and many were drag queens. While the participation of several Puerto Rican drag queens in the riots has been incorporated, albeit reluctantly, into the lore of Stonewall, the lesbian presence at Stonewall remains contested. Thus Duberman, for example, states that according to one view, the arrest of a cross-dressed lesbian (and her violent resistance) was the incident precipitating the riots, while other accounts firmly deny that a lesbian was even present in the bar.[55] This issue may never be settled, but the dispute says much about the creation of the myth.

In fact, the mythological construction of Stonewall may depend on the erasure of some of the people who were there. By erasing lesbians and people of color, the whitewashing of Stonewall invariably reduces gay history to the history of gay white men. The erasure is twofold. First there is the effacement of gender and race in accounts of the riots that mention neither that a large number of the patrons at the Stonewall Inn were Puerto Rican drag queens nor that it may well have been a lesbian, planting her foot in the chest of a police officer, who started the chain of resistance during the first night of the riots.

Equally significant, celebrating Stonewall as the birth of the gay movement eclipses the history of those who came to gay liberation via the civil rights struggle, those who, as it were, proclaimed that "black is beautiful" before they realized that "gay is good." Along similar lines, the exclusive focus on Stonewall erases female specificity by delegitimizing the accounts of lesbians who might trace their own origins back to the women's movement or lesbian feminism rather than to Stonewall. As John D'Emilio points out, "Lesbian-feminist organizations were filled with women who came not from the urban subculture of lesbian bars but from the heterosexual world, with the women's movement as a way station. As opponents of feminism were quick to charge, the women's movement was something of a 'breeding ground' for lesbianism."[56] The privileging of Stonewall thus highlights the gay movement's failure to acknowledge how race complicates questions of sexual identity and the difference that gender makes.

Queering the Stonewall Legend

The differences between a gay and a queer approach to history can be illustrated by comparing Martin Duberman's historical study *Stonewall* (1993) to Nigel Finch's film adaptation (1995), whose opening credits characterize it as a "fictionalisation based on the book by Martin Duberman." Duberman's book is a compilation of interviews with six individuals who came of age in the pre-Stonewall era and were drawn to the struggle for gay rights as a result of the upheaval at the Stonewall bar and the events that followed. According to Duberman, the book is an attempt to ground "the symbolic Stonewall in empirical reality" and to tell "for the first time the full story of what happened there."[57] The notion that one could establish a reliable historical narrative through interviews with people twenty-five years after the events they are being asked to recall seems somewhat naïve. As one critic puts it, "Like documenting a car crash, it's tough to get stories to match."[58] More important, however, Duberman's ideal of an exhaustive and definitive account of the Stonewall Riots evokes a specifically modernist sense of historiography, both in its dream of a "total history" and in its appeal to a Rankean ideal of objectivity.[59]

As Dominick LaCapra argues, the "dream of a 'total history' corroborating the historian's own desire for mastery of a documentary repertoire and furnishing the reader with a vicarious sense of—or perhaps a project for—control in a world out of joint" has been one of the guiding principles of modernist history.[60] Whereas poststructuralist theory has influenced other disciplines substantially, history initially remained impervious to it. The historian Hayden White has been especially critical of his profession and its steadfast refusal to critique its own practices. White suggests that history is "perhaps the conservative discipline par excellence" and accuses his colleagues of affecting a "kind of willful methodological naiveté" that for a long time allowed the profession to avoid any critical self-analysis.[61]

In the case of Duberman's study, published in the 1990s, this assessment raises the question of whether his appeal to empirical reality and his promise to tell the "full story" still have any persuasive relationship to contemporary theories of history and representation that have cast doubt on any text's ability to represent things as they are or, in the case of history, as they were. Over the course of the past twenty-five years or so, many—including a good number of theoretically sophisticated advocates of the so-called new history, such as LaCapra, White, and Joan W. Scott—have argued that historians need to respond creatively to challenges in contemporary thought and to learn from disciplines such as literary criticism, critical theory, and philosophy, where recent debates over the nature of interpretation have been particularly dynamic.[62] This engagement with theoretical advances in other disciplines and the willingness to develop a "'dialogical' exchange both with the past and with others inquiring into it," they argue, would allow historians to reformulate historiography "not simply as a repository of facts or a neo-positivistic stepchild of social science, and certainly not as a mythologized locus for some prediscursive image of 'reality,' but as a critical voice in the disciplines addressing problems of understanding and explanation."[63] The past, they contend, does not exist apart from consciousness of it. Consequently, facts are not discovered by the historian but rather constituted by the historian's inquiry. It is therefore not helpful to posit some histories as "objective" and others as not. Rather, students of history need to examine the subjectivity of *all* history and historians and the factors that influence their perspectives.

Such change, however, has been slow in developing. Perhaps one reason historians have largely been antagonistic to poststructuralist theory is that it seems to lead to the kind of relativism that undermines the historian's role as an objective arbiter of truth and reality. Duberman's book constitutes a case in point: his virtually unbroken belief that the historian discovers facts and that history conveys an objective truth can be sustained only by ignoring the postmodern arguments that, as Bravmann notes, "encourage an incredulity towards meta-narratives, trouble closure and resolution, valorize instability, and remain suspicious of coherence."[64] Duberman's book ignores these postmodern challenges in favor of an ideally exhaustive and definitive history that eschews any critical reflection on its own methodology and ideological implications.

In contrast to Duberman's book, Nigel Finch's film adaptation offers a specifically postmodern treatment of history, characterized by a clear emphasis on the individual who generates the film's historical narrative as well as significant doubts concerning our ability to know the past as it really happened. The film frames its narrative using what looks like documentary footage of the riots and talking-head sequences of veterans (including the late transgender activist Sylvia Rivera, who is featured in Duberman's book, too) telling how the riots changed their lives. The potential authenticity of this material is deliberately undercut, however, by a framing device for the segment that immediately follows the "documentary" footage: the use of one of the film's fictive characters, a Puerto Rican drag queen extraordinaire called La Miranda (Guillermo Diaz), to narrate Finch's dramatization of the Stonewall Riots and the weeks leading up to the event. When the film was first released, one reviewer suggested that Finch's device makes it clear that "the facts might have come from Martin Duberman's nonfiction book 'Stonewall,' but we're in fantasy territory."[65] This misses the point, however, for what is at stake in the conversion of book into film is not so much a distinction between fact and fiction. Rather, this "shrewd, term-defining opening" immediately alerts the spectator to the fact that Finch's view of history differs decisively from that provided by Duberman's book.[66]

The difference between Duberman's and Finch's approaches to historical representation becomes apparent with La Miranda's first words. Directly addressing the camera, she tells the audience: "See, there's as many Stonewall stories as there's gay queens in New York, and that's a shitload of stories, baby. Everywhere you go in Manhattan or America or the entire damn world, you gonna hear some new legend. Well, this is my legend, honey. Okay? My Stonewall legend." Thus, right from the start, La Miranda refuses the easy distinction between fact and fantasy by assimilating history to other forms of narrative. History, she reminds us, tells stories and creates legends, thus calling our attention to the constructed nature of all representations of the past, however ostensibly accurate they might be. Like stories and legends, history is *made*, fabricated rather than found.

The film proper employs similar alienation effects to interrupt an otherwise fairly traditional, at times melodramatic narrative. *Stonewall*'s music, among other elements, demonstrates that the film does not aim to provide an authoritative or complete history. In addition, the film's otherwise realistic cinematography is at times replaced by more striking visuals: a series of lip-synching sequences in which a group of drag queens acts like a Greek chorus, commenting on the action of the film and singing appropriate girl-group songs. The film's story line centers on a country boy, Matty Dean (Frederick Weller), whom initial reviews described as a "Southern boy" or a "Midwesterner,"[67] following him from his arrival at the Port Authority bus terminal to his participation in the riots. Along the way he meets the drag queens who hang out at the Stonewall Inn; falls in love with one of them, the film's central consciousness, La Miranda; joins the Homophile Society, a group of homosexual men clearly based on the Mattachine Society; falls in love with Ethan, a member of the organization; and quite predictably ends up torn between two lovers. Importantly, however, La Miranda and Ethan represent not only different erotic choices but also political alternatives for the recent arrival from small-town America. Matty finds himself torn between the pragmatic, assimilationist approach of the Homophile Society and the in-your-face style of his drag queen friends. Some of the most interesting moments in *Stonewall* occur when the two worlds collide: "Often there is conflict and misunderstanding, yet sometimes, when the characters let down their guards, mutual respect is found."[68] Thus, when one of the drag queens finds herself dancing with the head of the Homophile Society, she tells him,

"Between you and me, I do salute you." He responds, "Between you and me, I'm honored."

The significance of scenes like this one, however, goes beyond the mere expression of mutual respect on a personal level. By showing pragmatists and radicals working together—as the dance scene suggests, not necessarily side by side but at times hand in hand—*Stonewall* refuses the facile division between pre-Stonewall assimilationism and post-Stonewall radicalism. The film version of *Stonewall* replaces the traditional narrative, which posits a succession of incompatible political styles, by demonstrating that conflicting modes of organizing, confrontation, and cultural politics could coexist before the riots—and, I might add, continue to coexist to the present day.[69]

The idea that a historical narrative does not exist apart from the consciousness that generates it is once again taken up at the end of the film, when La Miranda suggests that participation in today's version of the American dream requires a history, however one might come by it: "Everyone has their own Stonewall legend; that's mine. I maybe didn't get exactly every detail down perfect, but that's the story of my life, honey. What the hell, I am a drag queen, and we don't always deal in reality. You could say that we deal in something kinda realer. We deal in dreams. We're American as apple pie." Through La Miranda's qualification of her own account, Finch makes a provocative statement about representations of the past, for her drag ethos encapsulates the recognition that any historical representation is necessarily partial. The commentary at the beginning and the end of the film calls attention to the rhetorical construction of historical representations and the subjective processes by which people interpret the past; it refuses both a modernist notion of total history and a singular interpretation of the Stonewall Riots.

The differences between Duberman's book and Finch's film can thus be traced to the distinction between modernist and postmodernist attitudes toward the twin projects of history and representation. As Harriet Malinowitz argues, postmodern theory's "object is not simply to give 'silenced' discourses a chance to be heard; it is rather to expose the indeterminate and hybrid nature of all discourse, to prompt incendiary questions about what is wrong with pictures that present themselves as seamlessly composed."[70] In the case of history, those taking a modernist approach may be content with including voices heretofore excluded or marginalized, without questioning the process of writing history itself. By contrast, those adopting a postmodernist perspective remain skeptical of history as usual and foreground the stakes involved in historical representation. Bravmann explains it thus: "As postmodern practices that suspend the search for historical certainty, the reading strategies of queer cultural studies of history mark a shift away from the residual empiricist impulse to determine *what* the past means for lesbians and gay men while turning towards the substantially greater instability of *how* the past's multiple textualizations construct meaning for queer historical subjects."[71] In other words, the queer is postmodern in its premise that truth is always contingent on context and positionality.

If queer is to gay and lesbian as postmodern is to modern, Nigel Finch's adaptation of *Stonewall* is both queer and postmodern insofar as it eschews Duberman's belief in empirical reality and cheerfully abandons the quest for a total history that would provide us with an objective, reliable, and definitive narrative of what happened at Stonewall. As Bravmann argues, "the powerful 'common sense' fiction that 'we' share at least some common goals—goals that are symbolically represented by the resistance during the riots—is one centrally problematic way Stonewall erases and creates historical memory, in regard to relations between gay men and lesbians as well as racial and political differences."[72] Finch's film version of *Stonewall* troubles this fiction of a unitary community with a shared history.

Finally, it is important to remember that the continued struggle over the meanings attributed to Stonewall is not an arcane matter of historiography; it is because "'the past' has this living active existence in the present that it matters so much politically."[73] To be sure, traditional gay mythologies of Stonewall have enabled both a notion of community and a particular kind of political organizing, most powerfully associated with the annual marches and gay pride celebrations commemorating the anniversary of the riots. Nevertheless, this kind of political mobilization has been based on the rhetorical positioning of Stonewall as an originary historical moment that implies that all gays and lesbians are fundamentally alike and share a common history—an account that, as I have demonstrated, ignores questions of race, gender, and other categories of difference. Finch's *Stonewall* makes a substantially different sort of sense of the riots in that La Miranda's history writes race, gender, and class into her account of the riots to enable a future politics that includes people of color, women, and those "fringe elements" of the community symbolized by the figure of the drag queen. While we may not be able to simply "forget Stonewall," as the title of this chapter polemically suggests, we need to question the notion that it has some kind of settled, definitive meaning. A greater number of queer fictions of the past will allow us not only to acknowledge the diversity that exists among queer historical subjects but also to proliferate the number of approaches to the project of GLBT liberation.

2

Queering the Rhetoric of the
Gay Male Sex Wars

Today any discussion of sex and sexuality will necessarily include an analysis of the public response to AIDS, for since the 1980s the HIV epidemic has become a "primary site for Americans to struggle over sexual ethics—to clarify the meaning and morality of sex."[1] The epidemic heightened Americans' feelings about sexuality in general. Not surprisingly, the meaning and public role of homosexuality were particularly contested, and gay men in the United States were faced with the threat that movements to restrict sexual expression in the wake of AIDS would be especially repressive of nonnormative sexualities. Thus, the advent of AIDS, as well as the public reaction to it, was a defining moment for gay men in the United States and soon became a central event in the construction of gay history. Michael Denneny, an author and influential editor of gay fiction for St. Martin's Press, argued in an essay first published in 1990 that "the history of the liberated gay community in America is divided into two phases": first, the construction of "a self-acknowledged community, initiated by the Stonewall riots in June 1969," and second, the years following the advent of the AIDS epidemic, which threatened to "destroy this community both physically and spiritually."[2] In fact, by the end of the 1980s many gay men saw the beginning of the epidemic as an event that rivaled the Stonewall Riots in historical significance.[3]

In this chapter I explore the continued struggle over the meaning of gay sexuality in the context of a reified division of recent history, with one era known as "post-Stonewall" or "pre-AIDS" (1969 to approximately 1982) and the other era, since the advent of the HIV epidemic in the early 1980s, designated somewhat misleadingly as the "post-AIDS" period. This before-and-after-AIDS model of gay history, I will demonstrate, has notably influenced debates among gay men over the significance of the epidemic itself as well as over the very meaning and morality of gay sex—a discussion that has found some of its most powerful expressions in the literature and cultural criticism produced by gay male writers. In the previous chapter I argued that the binary structure of before-and-after historical models makes meaning possible while simultaneously limiting the meanings we can make, and I analyzed both the cultural and political work these binary oppositions have *enabled* and the kinds of work they have *precluded.* Now I turn to a discussion of the way before-and-after models of history work in conjunction with either/or approaches to gay male sexuality, with one binary model reinforcing the other. Because debates among gay writers about gay male sexuality have been polarized, and at times virulent, I call the deeply entrenched conflict that pits "sex-positive" gay men against "sex-negative" ones the "gay male sex wars."[4]

Staking Out Positions in the Gay Male Sex Wars

Perhaps the most striking feature of gay literary representations of the epidemic, and of many gay novels dealing with AIDS in particular, has been what Michiko Kakutani, book critic for the *New York Times,* calls their "predictable architecture," that is, the way these stories and novels neatly divide into two periods: before and after AIDS.[5] In this context it is interesting to note that literature mirrors both (gay) history's somewhat arbitrary method of creating historical periods and the way HIV-positive people, particularly those infected early on, make meaning of the epidemic. Individuals living with HIV or AIDS frequently report that they experienced their diagnosis as a turning point, a landmark, as it were, that divided their life into two distinct and irreconcilable parts: health and sickness. *Borrowed Time,* Paul Monette's AIDS memoir, for instance, chronicles the life and death of his longtime companion, Roger Horrowitz. In his account of their life together, Monette conjures up "the time before the sickness" or "the time before the war," which ended abruptly on the day of Roger's diagnosis, the moment they "began to live on the moon."[6] The movement from health to sickness is completed by death and can be extended beyond it only figuratively: *Afterlife,* the novel that followed *Borrowed Time,* tells the stories of three AIDS widowers who embark on a life after AIDS.

The contrast between "pre-AIDS" and "post-AIDS" gay life is made even more explicit in David B. Feinberg's *Eighty-Sixed* (1989). The first half of the novel, titled "1980: Ancient History," documents protagonist B. J. Rosenthal's unsuccessful attempts to find a boyfriend in the gay world of New York City. Feinberg satirizes gay life in urban America at the beginning of the decade—a world of bathhouses, bars, and one-night stands. The novel's second part, "1986: Learning How to Cry," which is decidedly different in tone, depicts a drastically changed world—a world defined by such concerns as T-cell counts, night sweats, and Kaposi's sarcoma.[7]

In such memoirs and fiction life and death, sickness and health, are separated by the acronym AIDS and the so-called opportunistic infections associated with it. In a different way, however, the conceptual binary oppositions between life and death and sickness and health seem quite intimately linked as well to one thing whose meaning has changed quite dramatically since the advent of AIDS: sex. As John M. Clum argues in an article on the literature of the epidemic, AIDS "throws into question the values of the 1970s, the decade that Paul Monette calls 'the time before the war.'"[8] Consequently, AIDS narratives written by gay writers frequently focus not so much on the disease itself but on the author's or a character's changed relationship to his sexual past. B. J. Rosenthal, the narrator-protagonist of *Eighty-Sixed*, sums up how his recently acquired knowledge about HIV infection has changed his attitude toward sex: "These days, when you sleep with someone, you sleep with every one of his partners for the last five years, which makes for quite an orgy in my book—considering that in all likelihood some of the past partners are now dead. Erica Jong's zipless fuck has gone the way of the Edsel. There is no such thing as sex without angst anymore. The specter of death cannot be ignored, forgotten."[9] Because of AIDS, Feinberg's protagonist suggests, sex and death are inextricably linked, and the past, the time before AIDS, now seems remote.

Another revealing example of the linkage between sex and death that one can find in gay male writing is Oscar Moore's literary debut, *A Matter of Life and Sex*. By substituting the word *sex* for *death* in the familiar phrase "a matter of life and death," the novel's title not only establishes an intimate link between sex and death but seems to suggest that the two are interchangeable, that ultimately sex = death. This suggestion in turn provides a certain narrative logic to a novel that, according to the cover's synopsis, "charts one young man's journey into the soul and sex of gay life," from the first stirrings of his adolescent libido—he loses his virginity at fourteen in a public restroom—to his eventual death from AIDS.[10] The trajectory from "the lure of anonymous, promiscuous 'unsafe' sex"[11]—as the sensationalistic blurb on the dust jacket puts it—to the protagonist's demise seems to be characterized by an inevitability not unlike that of classical tragedy. But what is the hero's tragic flaw? The fact that his sexual adventures lead to his downfall implies that it is his predilection for "unsafe" sex. This suggestion is, of course, marred by anachronism. For prior to the discovery of HIV, the opposition safe/unsafe sex did not exist at all or existed only in strictly heterosexual terms (in the distinction between using birth control or not).[12] To suggest that the protagonist's penchant for unsafe sex—rather than sex in general—was his tragic flaw is to attribute meanings to sex and sexual practices that simply were not available or applicable to gay men before the advent of AIDS.

This anachronism, however, is in no way limited to literary representations of the epidemic. On the contrary, it points to a much larger problem, for not just literature but virtually *all* AIDS discourses are characterized by a considerable slippage in terminology that evades the differences between potentially dangerous sexual practices and sex per se. This slippage operates, for example, in the by-now infamous exhortation by politicians and public-health officials that it is necessary to abstain from sex altogether to steer clear of AIDS—a perspective that defines sex itself, not just specific potentially risky sexual acts, as the danger to be avoided. In terms of HIV prevention, however, the call for abstinence has been about as useful as the catchphrase "Just Say No" has been in the "war on drugs."[13] Both approaches offer simplistic solutions to difficult and complex issues. This becomes evident if we compare the number of people who contracted the virus though sex to the great number of those who, in the early years of the epidemic, were infected through transfusions of contaminated blood.[14] We know that blood transfusions in and of themselves do not pose a medical danger, let alone inevitably lead to death. Consequently, nobody was urging the public to "just say no" to blood transfusions. In the case of sex, however, the distinctions between risky sexual acts, unprotected sex, and sex in general have become hazy, frequently resulting in the wholesale vilification of sex, which does little to fight the spread of HIV.

Literary representations of the epidemic by gay writers as diverse as Monette, Feinberg, and Moore all portray the past as irretrievably lost. Opinions differ widely, however, on what the past signifies—that is, on precisely what has been lost and what should be remembered. To some the past represents a hard-won sexual freedom threatened by the epidemic; to others the past symbolizes the excesses of "the gay community," overindulging in casual sex after a long period of repression. In the realm of gay cultural criticism, these conflicting views have escalated into a war of words. The debate over the best way to respond to the threat of AIDS has created two opposing factions among gays by further escalating long-standing conflicts about the significance and morality of gay sex. One group likes to think of itself as sex positive and counts among its members such renowned cultural critics as Douglas Crimp, John M. Clum, Michael Bronski, and Frank Browning. Although their works differ in tone and approach, all these writers share the belief that sexuality has played a central part in the construction and development of gay male culture and gay politics. These sex positives further unite in their vocal disagreement with the views of a group of writers and journalists whom they accuse of having a negative attitude toward sex in general and gay sex in particular.

The sex-negative camp, too, has a number of prominent spokespeople: the activist-writer Larry Kramer, the late Randy Shilts, Bruce Bawer, and Andrew Sullivan. These writers, collectively referred to as sex negative, downplay the significance of sex for gay lives and gay organizing.

The sex-negative critique of gay lifestyles and politics is often associated with the political movement commonly known as "gay conservatism." Vocal proponents of this philosophy include Bruce Bawer and Andrew Sullivan. According to Bawer and Sullivan, a "silent majority" of "mainstream gays," who are "virtually normal" (that is, virtually indistinguishable from heterosexual mainstream society), simply want a "place at the table" of American democracy, yet the "fringe elements of the gay population"—deviant, sex-obsessed "subculture-oriented gays"—continue to spoil their prospects of assimilation.[15] Thus, in a column written for the mainstream gay and lesbian news magazine *The Advocate,* the self-described "sex-negative" Bawer warns that sex (particularly promiscuous sex) frequently hinders promoting the "idea of the moral equivalence of gays and straights," because it supports the charge that homosexuals are "about lust" while heterosexuals are "about love."[16] Bawer explains: "I want gay kids to grow up knowing that, as wonderful as sex can be, gay identity amounts to more than belonging to a 'culture of desire.'"[17] While gay conservatism as an organized political movement may be a relatively recent phenomenon, the sex-negative views expressed by Sullivan and Bawer echo arguments made ten years earlier by other gay writers, including Larry Kramer, arguably the most prominent representative of the sex-negative faction.

Speaking about gay men, Kramer has said, "Sex is not the fabric holding our community together: that's a very questionable assumption indeed about our commonality. We must realize that we are much, much more, that we have a sense of self and identity and relating such as exists in any religion or philosophy or ethnic background, and in which sex plays no more a role than it does in heterosexual identity. And if it takes an emergency epidemic to teach us this lesson, then let this be one of life's ironies."[18] Kramer's comparison of gay and straight identities in terms of sexuality may appear quite egalitarian at first glance, but closer scrutiny shows it to be more than a little lopsided. Heterosexuality is frequently couched in language that tends to obfuscate its sexual dimension. The twin concepts of marriage and family, for instance, represent sexual unions purely in terms of kinship arrangements. Since gay men do not have access to these institutions, they tend to be perceived as exclusively sexual beings. Not allowed to marry, often outlawed by their families of origin and the "national family," and denied recognition of their partnerships and chosen families, gay men just have sex, lots of it—at least that's what most mainstream representations of "the gay lifestyle" would have us believe. Gay men thus far have not attained the legitimacy and respectability the terms *marriage* and *family* (supposedly) bestow on heterosexuals. Therefore, Kramer's comparison of gay and straight identities is misleading because it ignores structural imbalances between homosexuality and heterosexuality.

Kramer's second major point—that AIDS manifests the failure of an ideology and a way of life that gay men should have outgrown by now—represents a school of thought according to which "the suffering brought on by AIDS is made meaningful by rendering it as instigating a personal and social awakening and maturation."[19] In this ironic scenario AIDS helps one grow up—just in time to die. Beyond this bitter irony, what is particularly troubling about gay discourses such as Kramer's is that they appear to be virtually indistinguishable from mainstream discourses for which AIDS signifies the failure of the so-called sexual revolution as well as a shift toward more "traditional" values—values that are, not surprisingly, heterosexually encoded. Indeed, these gay discourses risk complicity with conservative moral rhetorics that represent AIDS as a just punishment for violating a natural order, whether legislated by God or by nature.

The sex-positive writer and activist Douglas Crimp vehemently rejects this view of AIDS, yet he, too, conceives of AIDS as offering a lesson. In his programmatic essay "How to Have Promiscuity in an Epidemic," he maintains that promiscuity can provide a glimpse of a truly liberated sexual desire. Consequently, he argues that "having learned to support and grieve for our lovers and friends; having joined the fight against fear, hatred, repression, and inaction; having adjusted our sex lives so as to protect ourselves and one another," it is now time to reclaim "our subjectivities, our communities, our culture . . . and our promiscuous love of sex."[20] Not content to merely affirm the past, Crimp urges gay men to re-create what he considers to be a particular way of life that has come under attack in post-AIDS America. Reclaiming their sexual culture while adapting sexual practices to the demands of safer sex, he claims, is a political responsibility for gay men in the face of a hostile mainstream society.

Crimp's assertive and positive rhetoric typifies radical gay discourses that see in AIDS not the failure of a lifestyle but the menace of a homophobic society still in the grip of ignorance and backward attitudes. Within this particular framework, AIDS is not interpreted as the antithesis of or negative counterpart to Stonewall. Instead of being understood as an event that threatens post-Stonewall gains, it is seen as an event whose significance parallels the *original* significance of the riots. Initially Stonewall signified resistance to authorities' policing and harassment of lesbians and gay men and thus became a symbol of gay militancy. Gay politics after Stonewall, albeit only for a short while, focused on analyzing and changing a homophobic society rather than on attempting to fit into that society. Radical gay activists see AIDS as they saw Stonewall: a critical turning point in gay politics, a phenomenon that should occasion broad social change.

In sharp contrast to Crimp, Scott Tucker, another sex-positive writer, categorically refuses to view AIDS as a blessing in disguise: "As William Blake wrote, 'Blight never does good to a tree . . . but if it still bear[s] fruit, let none say the fruit was in consequence of the blight.' [. . .] AIDS has provoked a crisis in our sexual and spiritual lives; the danger is that gay people will unwittingly accept the moral and political leadership of people who would prefer us back in the closet—or dead."[21] It is important to note that Tucker's caution applies not only to the religious right's reading of AIDS as God's *punishment* for the sin of homosexuality but also to Kramer's interpretation of the epidemic as a *lesson* for the gay community as well as to Crimp's notion of AIDS as an *occasion* for social change.

This conflict has been anything but academic and polite. Sex positives have frequently charged their opponents with internalized homophobia and delight in representing them as the ideological bedfellows of Jesse Helms, Pat Robertson, William F. Buckley, and Jerry Falwell, all of whom have referred to AIDS as God's punishment for gay promiscuity.[22] Sex negatives have accused sex positives of being immature and hopelessly stuck in the 1970s, unwilling to face the changed realities of post-AIDS America. Considering the high stakes in these gay sexuality debates, as well as the ideologically charged atmosphere in which they are taking place, the virulence of the conflict hardly seems surprising. More troubling, however, is that the deep divisions between the two entrenched camps leave little room for a discourse that avoids such polarization, especially since each side is also quite vehement in its demand for "positive representations" of the gay community, either as happily promiscuous or blissfully monogamous.

For instance, the sex-positive cultural critic John Clum argues that "affirming the past is affirming the power of sexual desire" and proclaims that "AIDS literature must deal with [such conflations as] past sexuality = present disease in a way that either breaks the chain or at least affirms the past in a healing way."[23] In other words, Clum insists that gay writing's core mission is to celebrate the sexual past and to defend it against any attempts to construct gay male sexuality as the cause of disease.

Given the misguided attempts to blame the epidemic on gay men and their sexual behavior in the 1970s, Clum's call for gay writers to challenge discourses that claim causal connections between promiscuity and AIDS, between gay sex and death, is all too understandable. At the same time, however, his view of gay writing is overly prescriptive, suggesting as it does that the function of gay writing, whether literature or cultural criticism, should be restricted to promoting a party line. As Philip Derbyshire points out, such a reductive view of writing risks "relegat[ing] cultural production to the realm of facile propagandism," for it "occludes discussion of actual contradictions within our lives."[24] Once the defense of gay promiscuity becomes official policy, any writer who so much as contemplates monogamy as a choice and does not come out squarely in defense of promiscuity automatically violates that policy. "If you're not with us, you're against us" is the not-so-subtle warning to any gay writer who might be inclined to take the road less traveled and explore alternatives beyond the hot-button issue of determining whether promiscuity is good or bad. This creates a highly polarized scenario in which it is virtually impossible to even think about monogamy as an option for gay men without being scorned by sex-positive gay writers.

The conflict between sex negatives and sex positives during the last two decades clearly reveals that both positions assume the mistaken notion that a social practice such as sex (which in and of itself is neither moral nor immoral) could be endowed with supposedly *essential* moral qualities. Because gay sex does not have any a priori qualities—because, in other words, it is neither essentially good nor essentially bad—the argument between sex positives and sex negatives amounts to little more than both sides declaring their deeply cherished beliefs. The result has been the breakdown of any kind of dialogue and a subsequent recourse to name calling and personal attacks.

A Queer Alternative to the Gay Male Sex Wars

One way to move beyond this impasse in the monogamy versus promiscuity debate can be found in *The Blue Lady's Hands,* the first novel by the writer and cultural critic John Champagne. This book's protagonist strives for his own definition of love and sex and insists on living homosexual desire according to what feels right to him—with all the uncertainties this entails—rather than accept the dogmas people seek to impose on him. Juxtaposing Champagne's early work to the late work of Michel Foucault, I will read the struggle of Champagne's protagonist for a position beyond the either/or propositions of the gay male sex wars as an encouraging example of something that in an interview Foucault once called a "homosexual mode of life," a space of personal and social transformation that we might more accurately describe as a *queer* way of life[25]—even though both the interview and the novel were published before this term was widely used in its current meaning.

More specifically, the queer alternative to the monogamy versus promiscuity debate Champagne develops in his novel exemplifies the kind of queer self-transformation Foucault had in mind when he referred to homosexuality as a "practice of the self" capable of constructing different ways of life. Foucault explained this idea in a seminar he gave at the University of Vermont in October 1982. He discussed the different "techniques" or "technologies" that human beings use to understand themselves: technologies of production, technologies of sign systems, technologies of power, and technologies of the self. He defines technologies of the self as those that "permit individuals to effect by their own means, or with the help of others, a certain number of operations on their own bodies and souls, thoughts, conduct, and a way of being, so as to transform themselves in order to attain a certain state of happiness."[26] Champagne has his protagonist engage in such a transformative practice, allowing him to develop what today we might call a queer relationship or a queer way of life.

Initially the nameless narrator in *The Blue Lady's Hands* is shown developing a blueprint for his own life based on his admiration for his parents' relationship. Thus, he starts his career as a gay man trying to emulate his parents' marriage. From their example he has gathered that sex should occur only in the context of a romantic relationship, which in turn should be based on the twin ideals of fidelity and monogamy. "I knew I was just like them," he states emphatically, "except I loved men instead of women"—not yet realizing that this "minor" detail can make a significant difference. Things change dramatically, however, when he meets Daniel, a man who not only has another lover who showers him with fan mail and gifts but also belongs to a jack-off club.[27] The protagonist has difficulty controlling his jealousy and freely admits that he is "afraid of losing [Daniel] to this club."[28] What is he to do when the man with whom he has fallen in love goes to a group masturbation party on a Saturday night? Champagne's novel focuses on what it means to live homosexual desire in the age of AIDS; at the heart of the novel is the protagonist's attempt to figure out how to realize his concept of love and sex in a relationship with a man whose ideas about these matters differ decidedly from his own.

Eschewing the supposedly absolute distinction between gay promiscuity and straight monogamy, the author chronicles his protagonist's development of a specifically *queer* position, one that not only combines elements of both perspectives but ultimately moves beyond them into uncharted territory. For instance, the either/or logic of the war between sex positives and sex negatives suggests that the renunciation of monogamy means the automatic embrace of promiscuity—and vice versa. *The Blue Lady's Hands,* however, demonstrates that a gay man's choices in the age of AIDS can be considerably more complex.

To broaden his exploration of sexuality, Champagne introduces two additional characters, the protagonist's friends Randy and Brian. As far as they are concerned, "monogamy is the invention of repressed Catholics who hate homosexuals," whereas sex is "a sport, meant to be enjoyed."[29] Both men proudly proclaim that they have been with hundreds of men and that monogamy has never been part of their relationship. As they explain to their doubting friend, "Since faggots are no good at sports, we have sex instead."[30] They tell him: "That is what being gay means—there are no rules. We are not our parents. Everyone has a right to determine how he will treat his own body. As long as no one gets hurt."[31]

The protagonist, however, refuses his friends' definition of sex as a purely recreational "sport" as well as their idea that monogamy entails repression and internalized homophobia. "Why is it okay for everyone to choose what he wants to do with his body except for me? If I choose monogamy, then I'm unnatural. It isn't fair."[32] He relates the charges leveled against him by Brian and Randy to the rejection of all gay people by heterosexuals: "I was told when I was younger that being gay was unnatural. Now I'm told by other

[gay] men that I'm unnatural because I don't want to sleep around."[33] In the final analysis, the protagonist disavows both fundamental monogamy and militant promiscuity. He rejects absolute positions, opting instead to formulate a situational ethics derived from "what takes place" between him and his partner.[34] As far as he is concerned, the fact that his parents' rules do not apply to his relationship with Daniel means not that there are no rules but rather that rules will inevitably differ depending on individual needs and situations. These rules have to be negotiated on a case-by-case basis rather than be handed down to the lovers through tradition. The protagonist concedes the uncertainty that this search for new ways of relating entails when he says: "I am not a saint. I am not perfect. I don't know if I can love someone who also loves somebody else."[35] Champagne's hero does not denounce either promiscuity or anonymous sex. While he chooses not to engage in these behaviors himself, he acknowledges that they are viable and healthy choices for other gay men—including his boyfriend.

Rather than join either the sex-positive or the sex-negative faction, Champagne's protagonist (and hence Champagne's readers) can thus deconstruct the terms of the war between the two camps. The protagonist undergoes a learning process, moving from an unreflective aping of heterosexual structures to an acceptance of his partner Daniel's promiscuity within the framework of safer sex.[36] "Maybe if it weren't for AIDS," he muses, "I'd be sleeping with strangers too."[37] Importantly, however, Champagne does not have his hero condemn promiscuity; instead, the author merely has him decide that, at least at this point in time, he prefers to be monogamous—even if that puts him in the paradoxical position of being in a monogamous relationship with a promiscuous man.

Sex positives such as Douglas Crimp rightly challenge the myth that "monogamous relationships are not only the norm but ultimately everyone's deepest desire."[38] By the same token, one might argue that promiscuity is not the gay man's norm or his deepest desire. As Scott Tucker points out, "Making a dogma of *non*monogamy is, of course, merely reactive and negative."[39] Crimp, however, does make a dogma of nonmonogamy by exhorting gay men to reclaim their "promiscuous love of sex." Like conservative rhetorics, Crimp's demand presents promiscuity as an essential trait shared by all homosexual men, implying that gay men are *by nature* promiscuous. In other words, Crimp's radical stance depends on the same essentialist definitions of gay promiscuity that characterize homophobic notions about homosexuality—including the assumption that, unlike heterosexuals, homosexuals are by nature promiscuous. By accepting the binary logic of gay promiscuity versus straight monogamy, pleasure versus responsibility, gay analyses of sexuality in the age of AIDS remain hopelessly embroiled in heterosexual and, more important, heterosexist cultural values. Homosexual desire, however, is not monolithic, and neither is the way that gay men express their desire.

As Champagne's work demonstrates, the two sides of the gay male sex wars hardly exhaust the possibilities. More important, Champagne's protagonist illustrates the idea that Foucault proposed in his late work on ethics and sexual morality in ancient Greece and Rome, a phenomenon he called "ascesis," or a "practice of the self"—working on the self to transform it into a source of independence and pleasure.[40] The kind of "ascetical practice" Foucault had in mind, however, has very little to do with the abnegation or renunciation of pleasure the term traditionally denotes. Rather, Foucault defines *ascesis* as "an exercise of self upon self by which one tries to work out, to transform one's self and to attain a certain mode of being."[41] Foucault came to understand both philosophy and homosexuality as modern versions of ascesis. In the introduction to *The Use of Pleasure* Foucault thus remarks that the task of redefining the self's relation to the self was a central motivation for his last investigations: "As for what motivated me [. . . ,] it was curiosity—the only kind of curiosity, in any case, that is worth acting upon with a degree of obstinacy: not the curiosity that seeks to assimilate what is proper for one to know, but that which enables one to get free of oneself. After all, what would be the value of the passion for knowledge if it resulted only in a certain amount of knowledgeableness and not, in one way or another to the extent possible, in the knower's straying afield of himself?"[42] This straying afield of oneself is programmatic in that it constitutes a transformative test the philosopher performs on him- or herself by playing games of truth. "What is philosophy today," Foucault asks, "if it is not the critical work that thought brings to bear on itself? In what does it consist, if not in the endeavor to know how and to what extent it might be possible to think differently, instead of legitimating what is already known?"[43] He goes on to remark that the living substance of philosophy is still "what it was in times past, i.e., an 'ascesis,' *askésis,* an exercise of oneself in the activity of thought."[44] The ultimate goal of this exercise is to change one's self, to get away from the self, by "think[ing] differently than one thinks, and perceiv[ing] differently than one sees."[45]

Foucault thought about homosexuality in much the same way. In an interview with a French gay magazine, he denounced the "tendency to relate the question of homosexuality to the problem of 'Who am I?' and 'What is the secret of my desire?' Perhaps it would be better to ask oneself, 'What relations, through homosexuality, can be established, invented, multiplied and modulated?' The problem is not to discover in oneself the truth of sex but rather to use sexuality henceforth to arrive at a multiplicity of relationships."[46] Gays, according to Foucault, had to do more than assert an identity; they had to create it, and its creation was by no means equivalent to the liberation of an essence. Therefore, he concluded, "we have to work at *becoming homosexual* and not be obstinate in recognizing that we are."[47] Glossing Foucault's statement, David Halperin suggests that Foucault actually meant that gays have to work on *becoming queer*. He explains that "one can't *become* homosexual, strictly speaking: one either is or one isn't. But one can marginalize oneself; one can transform oneself; one can become queer. Indeed, 'queer' marks the very site of gay becoming."[48] It is precisely such a queer transformative practice that the nameless protagonist of *The Blue Lady's Hands* develops.

Foucault claims that what makes homosexuality disturbing is less the sexual act itself than the "homosexual mode of life"—which, following Halperin, we might call a queer way of life: "To imagine a sexual act that doesn't conform to law or nature is not what disturbs people. But that individuals are beginning to love one another—there's the problem."[49] Foucault therefore rejects the reduction of homosexuality to sexual acts, which appears commonly in both straight attacks on gay promiscuity and gay defenses of promiscuity and anonymous sex. Such a reductionism, Foucault maintains, "annuls everything that can be uncomfortable in affection, tenderness, friendship, fidelity, camaraderie and companionship, things which our rather sanitized society can't allow a place for without fearing the formation of new alliances and the tying together of unforeseen lines of force."[50] In other words, the terror of homosexual sex masks a "more profound anxiety about a threat to the way people are expected to relate to one another, which is not too different from saying the way power is positioned and exercised in our society."[51] But Foucault does not pit sexuality against relationality. On the contrary, as Leo Bersani points out, Foucault implies that "a new lifestyle, new kinds of relationship, are indissociable from new sex acts—or, in his preferred terms, from a new economy of bodily pleasures."[52] Consequently, the task of elaborating a queer way of life is a matter of "fabricating other forms of pleasure, of relationships, coexistences, attachments, loves, intensities."[53] Becoming queer, then, means developing decidedly different relational systems through sexual practices.

When Champagne's protagonist announces, "I learned [. . .] that my life wasn't going to be like anyone else's, least of all my parents',"[54] he is taking a first step toward negotiating the meaning of his relationship in the absence of any established codes or guidelines. At the same time, however, he also rejects his friends' definition of sex as a purely recreational sport: "I am not my parents. But I am also not Randy and Brian."[55] This statement of the narrator's sexual independence indicates what Foucault terms the queer subject's attempt to "escape the two ready-made formulas of the pure sexual encounter and the lovers' fusion of identities."[56] In Champagne's fiction it is up to the protagonist and his partner to develop their own relationship by discovering what is appropriate in their situation, independent of the models of heterosexual monogamy and homosexual promiscuity presented to them by the protagonist's parents and his gay friends, respectively.

What makes these characters' negotiations so difficult, in addition to the lack of established codes and models already mentioned, is the inclusion of another person—Daniel's "secret admirer"—as well as Daniel's refusal to give up his participation in jack-off parties for the sake of the relationship. As Champagne's novel demonstrates, inventing queer relationships ultimately means confronting what Foucault posits as the fundamental question: "How is it possible for men to be together? To live together, to share their time, their meals, their room, their leisure, their grief, their knowledge, their confidences? What is it to be 'naked' among men, outside of institutional relations, family, profession and obligatory camaraderie?"[57] Queerness thus has the potential to reorganize dominant definitions of intimacy. Foucault points out the possibility that "changes in established routines will occur on a much broader scale as gays learn to express their feelings for one another in more various ways and develop new life-styles not resembling those that have been institutionalized."[58]

Developments since the mid-1990s seem to attest to Foucault's prescience. For example, queer activists and writers have argued that primary relationships may involve more than two people and thereby completely rewrite the social conventions of "the couple." What Foucault did not foresee, however, is that the major impetus for this massive redefinition of relationality is coming from lesbians and bisexual women and not, as he had predicted, from gay men. One reason for this may be that lesbian and gay sexuality are currently evolving in different directions. As Marcia Munson and Judith Stelboum remark, "In the 1980s, as lesbians and gay men joined forces to fight AIDS, many lesbians were influenced by gay men's freer, more exotic, and playful sexual style. This happened at the same time that many gay men saw health reasons to curb their uninhibited sexuality. [. . .] In the 1990s, we hear[d] gay men promoting monogamy as a way to gain acceptability in mainstream culture."[59] Gabriel Rotello's *Sexual Ecology* and Michelangelo Signorile *Life*

Outside provide examples of gay writers promoting pair bonding by present-ing nonmonogamous behavior as infantile and dangerous. While these gay writers tried—once again—to coerce gay men into respectable, marriage-like monogamous relationships, others reacted to this most recent outburst of sex negativity by proclaiming—once again—the intrinsic worth of promis-cuity.

Thus gay authors largely remained embroiled in the monogamy versus promiscuity debate,[60] whereas scores of lesbian writers sought alternatives to this oversimplified dichotomy. Books such as Dossie Easton and Catherine A. Liszt's *Ethical Slut: A Guide to Infinite Sexual Possibilities* and Celeste West's *Lesbian Polyfidelity* push the postmodern politics of pleasure by exploring nonstandard lifestyles frequently grouped together under the heading "poly-amory." As Munson and Stelboum note in their introduction to the recent *Lesbian Polyamory Reader,* the term *polyamory* includes "many different styles of multiple intimate involvements, such as polyfidelity or group marriage; primary relationships open to secondary affairs; and casual sexual involve-ment with two or more people."[61] These elaborations of queer relationality beyond marriage on the one hand and anonymous sex on the other become a mode of personal and social transformation and have the potential of inventing a queer way of life.

Rhetorical Reification and the Need to Queer the Discourse

As I mentioned earlier in this chapter, sex positives have frequently charged sex-negative writers and activists such as Larry Kramer with internalized homophobia. David Bergman, however, correctly points out the emptiness of such a charge against Kramer: "Just as no American is free of racism, so, too, no one is free of internalized homophobia."[62] Sex positives who attempt to link the rhetoric of, say, Larry Kramer with that of, say, Jerry Falwell are primarily motivated by the desire to discredit their opponents by associating them with enemies of the gay community. No matter how successful this strategy may have been in the gay male sex wars, it should not blind us to the fact that the religious right's response to the AIDS epidemic has obviously been very different, both in motivation and effect, from that of gay activists, be they sex negative or sex positive.

That being said, religious conservatives and gay activists of both stripes sometimes construct their arguments about the social effects of AIDS in disturbingly similar ways. Rather than look at the personal predisposition of individual authors, it might be more productive to analyze the rhetorical model that people of different political persuasions use in constructing their arguments. This rhetorical analysis may help explain how, despite their fundamentally different assessments of the epidemic, a gay activist and an antigay conservative can sound so alarmingly alike. Rhetorical forms control and restrict how we can approach a particular question, what we can say about a particular topic. Such restrictions are particularly significant when it comes to AIDS discourse, for as I have argued elsewhere, "the meanings we attribute to AIDS shape the reality of living with AIDS."[63]

Ultimately the eerie similarity between the discourse of gay activists and that of religious conservatives results directly from their use of the same rhetorical mode when writing about the epidemic: the religious right and gay activists narrate the history from Stonewall to AIDS according to the same historical model—the jeremiad—using (variations of) the same rhetorical approach to make their respective points. The term *jeremiad* refers to a sermon or other composition that accounts for an era's misfortunes as a just penalty for great moral and social evils while holding out hope for changes that will bring a happier future. It derives from the Old Testament prophet Jeremiah, who in the seventh and sixth centuries B.C. attributed the calamities of Israel to its abandonment of the covenant with Jehovah and its return to pagan idolatry. Jeremiah called on the people to repent and reform so that Jehovah might restore them to his favor and renew the ancient covenant. Puritans adapted this form to conditions in the New World and developed the prototype of what eventually became a specifically American form of the jeremiad. As Emory Elliott points out in the *Cambridge History of American Literature,* "taking their texts from Jeremiah and Isaiah, these orations followed—and reinscribed—a rhetorical formula that included recalling the courage and piety of the founders, lamenting recent and present ills, and crying out for a return to the original conduct and zeal. In current scholarship, the term 'jeremiad' has expanded to include not only sermons but also other texts that rehearse the familiar tropes of the formula."[64]

To recognize conservative interpretations of AIDS as a contemporary version of the American jeremiad, we need to consider them in the broader context of the religious right's reaction to the social upheavals of the 1960s and 1970s, which certain segments of the American population perceived as confusing and threatening. This "social revolution" comprised rapid technological advances; a dramatically changing world economy; and changes in race relations, gender roles, and sexual mores, exemplified by, among other things, the struggle over civil rights, the Equal Rights Amendment, and the changing status of homosexuality. Analyzing the rise of televangelism and religious fundamentalism, Michael D'Antonio notes that conservative Christianity began to flourish at the very moment when "more moderate and liberal denominations, which recognized the complexities of modern life and resisted biblical simplification, declined."[65] According to D'Antonio, what ultimately proved so compelling to the millions who turned to evangelical Christianity was "its promise of unalterable truths and its nostalgia for a simpler past."[66]

The "unalterable truths" that allowed right-wing Christianity to circumvent the seemingly confounding complexities of modern life resulted from a recourse to pre-Enlightenment models of historiography, providing typological interpretations of history that categorize historical occurrences according to (supposedly) eternal models. As D'Antonio explains, Jerry Falwell and other conservative evangelicals "applied the Bible to what they saw and argued that the confusion and problems of American life—from economic recession to herpes—were the penalty for 'turning away from God.'"[67] According to this logic, the troubling realities of the times were God's punishment for the *national* sins perpetrated by feminism, the civil rights movement, and the "homosexual revolution." It is the emphasis on the fate of the nation that squarely places this rhetoric in the tradition of the American jeremiad, which Sacvan Bercovitch defines as "a mode of public exhortation" designed to "join social criticism to spiritual renewal, public to private identity, the shifting 'signs of the times' to certain traditional metaphors, themes, and symbols."[68]

In the 1980s AIDS could easily be read as one of the "signs of the times" that were supposed to illustrate the connections between public and private identities. The religious right viewed AIDS as symbolizing the failure of social liberalization and as a just punishment for the permissiveness and sexual experimentation of the 1960s and 1970s. Soon this perspective found broader acceptance in conservative circles beyond the religious right. Thus, while the epidemic did not produce any new conservative discourses on homosexuality as such, it without doubt gave renewed impetus to traditional conservative discourses that portray eros and romance as inseparable, valorize monogamy, and represent homosexuality as the antithesis of the heterosexual ideal. In the particular case of AIDS, "conservatives point to the divorce of desire from love as the very root of the perverse and promiscuous nature of homosexuality, which links it to disease and death."[69] According to a literally Puritanical way of thinking that sees outward states (e.g., symptoms of disease) as symbolizing inward ones (e.g., spiritual malaise), the visible manifestations of AIDS became signs of a diseased, abnormal, and socially dangerous sexual desire. Ultimately, the recourse to AIDS was merely the latest in a long line of conservatives' attempts to delegitimize homosexuality by representing the homosexual as a dangerous and polluted figure and the gay male body as always already diseased. AIDS seemed to prove a kind of "truth" about homosexuality and homosexuals that hitherto could be known only intuitively. In the words of an anonymous surgeon quoted in *Let the Record Show,* ACT UP's indictment of "AIDS criminals": "We used to hate faggots on an emotional level. Now we have a good reason."[70]

Of particular interest here is the conservatives' tendency to read the epidemic as a symptom of the decline of values they cherish. This rhetoric advocates a return to the "old ways," some supposedly originary state that, as it happens, coincides with the moral or political position of these self-announced chroniclers of moral decay. In their constructions of AIDS, conservatives thus narrate the ensuing cultural decline to reaffirm their hegemony. AIDS, in other words, gets reinscribed in a very old story whose reiteration helps consolidate dominant cultural forces.

As Bercovitch and others have demonstrated, if a narrative is to have value in the public domain, it must be perceived as making *moral* judgments that subsequently become the legitimate grounds on which *political* action can be taken. There must be a relationship between representations of moral difference and political action. In narrative the motivation behind the representation of moral difference is the desire to intervene in a real situation and to legitimize this intervention through the narrative provided. Moral distinctions in a dominant discourse help to facilitate an ideological consensus that then allows actions against groups and individuals who are now seen as worthy targets because of their immorality.

As has been true for older versions of this rhetorical strategy, if this latest incarnation of the American jeremiad is to become an effective tool in the struggle for political hegemony, the enumeration of sins and sinners must be coupled with "the promise of redemption,"[71] a belief in that pillar of the American dream valued since the Puritans, the doctrine of progress. For fundamentalists, atonement for the sins of the 1960s and 1970s requires America to return to the Christian values of a simpler, more stable time. This involves not only the renunciation of homosexuality as a legitimate "lifestyle" but also a full-fledged "return to the patriotic style of the Cold War era and to highly conservative domestic policies."[72] As D'Antonio explains, "That meant, among others things, a renewed ban on abortion, a constitutional amendment to reinstitute school prayer, a military buildup to recapture the nation's strategic dominance, and censorship to outlaw pornography."[73] Just as the assessment of the country's malaise had been based on the literal interpretation of scripture, the suggested remedy sought to reform America by reinstating Bible-based law. In the 1980s, however, with courts refusing to overturn *Roe v. Wade* and overwhelming public support for legal abortion, gay-bashing overtook opposition to abortion as "the best way to rally the Religious Right, the GOP's core constituency."[74] This strategy determined conservative politics until the American voting public resoundingly rejected it in the 1992 election. Ironically, the most extreme expression of this strategy also marked the beginning of its demise. At the 1992 Republican National Convention, the conservative Republican Pat Buchanan tried to enlist delegates for his "holy war," telling them that gay rights had no place "in a nation we still call God's country."[75] His call to arms was rejected not only by mainstream Republicans but also by a majority of the electorate who perceived the GOP to be too much under the influence of the religious right.

In the fall of 2001 it became clear that in attempts to explain the "signs of the times," the American jeremiad still was a favorite. In the speech he delivered at the National Cathedral on 14 September 2001, the National Day of Prayer and Remembrance, Billy Graham tried to make sense of what had happened in New York, Washington, and rural Pennsylvania three days earlier. "Difficult as it may be for us to see right now," he said, "this event can give a message of hope—hope for the present, and hope for the future." Graham elaborated: "There is hope for the present because I believe the stage has already been set for a new spirit in our nation. One of the things we desperately need is a spiritual renewal in this country. We need a spiritual revival in America. And God has told us in His Word, time after time, that *we are to repent of our sins and we are to turn to Him and He will bless us in a new way.*"[76] In typical jeremiad fashion, this passage joins social criticism to the promise of spiritual renewal as it promises God's blessing in return for our repentance.

Graham's speech and the message of hope it contained were well received. A quite different reception, however, awaited a specific application of the ideas expressed in this sermon: Jerry Falwell's now-infamous outburst on Pat Robertson's *700 Club* blaming the terrorist assault of 9/11 on gays, lesbians, and others who "have tried to secularize America." As an article in *The Advocate* reports, the political left "swiftly expressed collective disgust" with Falwell's assertion that gay people, among others, helped set the stage for the attacks.[77] Perhaps more surprising, several of the evangelist's past political allies took issue with Falwell's remarks as well. Commentators from Arianna Huffington to Rush Limbaugh distanced themselves from Falwell, as did a spokesperson for the White House, who made a point of telling the press that President Bush does not share these views. Such presidential criticism, however, did not inaugurate a change in the political climate. On the contrary, in the 2004 election "moral issues" such as the ones addressed by Falwell mobilized a significant number of evangelical Christian voters, who subsequently claimed that they had been instrumental in securing President Bush's reelection, making the president considerably more cautious not to alienate members of the religious right, no matter how extreme the views they expressed.

In *Cities on a Hill* Frances FitzGerald argues that "the politics of the New Right is, in great degree, merely the overflow of [. . .] fundamentalism from the churches into the public domain."[78] One reason the religious right gained such a strong foothold in the 1980s is the narrative power of the biblical model on which conservatives fashioned their latter-day jeremiads: the fall from innocence and grace. The notion of a fall from grace not only figures prominently in Christian mythology but also has provided perhaps one of the main paradigms of Western historiography. In religious discourse sexuality is represented as the act that inevitably leads to the Fall and thus comes to signify both the difference between God and human beings and the difference between good and evil. This narrative of the Fall as brought about by sex in turn becomes the legitimating discourse that historically has allowed the church to discipline bodies. Surprisingly, perhaps, this model has remained virtually unchanged in the transition from theology to history. An analysis of historical accounts of the period from Stonewall to AIDS proves particularly instructive about the way historiography employs religious models to tell a tale and to adorn a moral.

In shading theology into history, a preliminary step involves establishing the kind of historical model I analyzed in chapter 1, in which certain pivotal events divide a span of time into discrete periods of before and after. Social practices—sexuality, for example—can then be reified by plugging them into this rigid before-and-after model of history: they are essentialized through their association with what is figured as a unified historical period. Promiscuity, for example, becomes the essence of post-gay-liberation homosexuality. Indeed, in conservative accounts of recent history, the post-Stonewall period is represented as essentially promiscuous, while the post-AIDS years are considered to mark a return to the state of affairs before that pivotal moment in 1969. What the theological model gives historiography is a gloss on discontinuity that reads the discontinuity in moral terms: a sequence that moves from a before to an after signifies not merely change but rather a particular moral pattern. In the area of moral instruction, history comes to assume functions that religion used to perform by establishing an explicitly moral relationship between past and present. As a way of making meaning of the world, history ultimately replaces religion.

These religious underpinnings of historical approaches to the recent past suggest that the similarities between gay analyses of sexuality in the age of AIDS and the religious right's ideas about homosexuality may indicate not merely internalized homophobia in the former but a similar rhetoric in both. For instance, both conservative responses and responses by sex-negative gay writers are couched in rhetoric indebted to the model of the Fall. Of course, the two sides deploy this biblical prototype in crucially different ways. As far as the religious right is concerned, the only form of redemption available to homosexual sinners is being born again—as Christian *and* as straight.[79] For their part, gay writers from Kramer and Shilts to Bawer and Sullivan emphasize the necessity of reevaluating the significance we ascribe to sex, in the lives of gay men and in gay organizing, so that "the gay community" can emerge strong and rejuvenated from the AIDS crisis. Unlike conservative readings of the epidemic that derive their moral imperative from visions of a paradise lost, these gay responses instead focus on the promise of a paradise to be regained.

Indeed, the fact that gay writing often confers redemptive significance on AIDS as a catalyst for the rebirth of a supposed gay community may suggest that the only structural difference between these gay representations of the epidemic and the ideology of the new right consists in a disagreement over the telos of history—destruction or renewal—or the distinction between a vengeful and a forgiving God. It would of course be ludicrous to suggest that gay writers accept the religious right's condemnation of the gay community (or their apparent glee at what fundamentalists believed to be its imminent destruction). Nevertheless, gay writers unfortunately restrict their own argumentative strategies when they latch onto a rhetorical model that is already being exploited by their detractors. Importantly, these gay writers do not displace the model of the Fall; they merely reiterate that model in the redemptive mode. Changing the telos of history does not nullify the moral charge of the model of the Fall, no matter what we take to be its ultimate outcome.

Sex-positive gay writers categorically reject the idea that there is a moral message to be learned from AIDS, yet they, too, present AIDS as an occasion for change. Crimp, for example, argues that gay men should respond to the antisex, antigay ideas that dominate mainstream discourses on AIDS by unapologetically asserting their sexuality and defending their right to promiscuity. Crimp is hopeful that the reactionary backlash triggered by AIDS will once again radicalize the gay movement, bringing it closer to the kind of militant, antihomophobic politics the Stonewall Riots once symbolized. The very idea of *renewal*, of course, is an integral part of the jeremiad's rhetorical strategy. Importantly, for Crimp the Fall is evidenced not by the epidemic itself but by mainstream society's callous and brutally homophobic reaction to AIDS. Not underestimating this crucial distinction, it nonetheless must be pointed out that Crimp's argument is severely restricted because he uses the same biblical model for making meaning of the world that the religious right and sex-negative gay writers use.

Crimp himself comments on the crucial connections between content and form in his critique of the sex-negative writers Kramer and Shilts, in which he rightly points out that "cultural conventions rigidly dictate what can and will be said about AIDS."[80] Sex-positive writers are subject to the same limitations, of course, and in an ironic way Crimp proves his own point through his failed attempt to employ the rhetorical form of the jeremiad to further a gay radical politics. The fact that the same rhetorical model has been employed by not only the religious right but also sex-negative *and* sex-positive gay writers to forward diametrically opposed political agendas casts doubt on the notion that antihegemonic cultural and political work can be done, and done effectively, within the constraints of established rhetorical conventions. Crimp may be able to reverse the discourse by arguing that, contrary to what the religious right has claimed, gay promiscuity is a good thing and can lead to positive results, yet this does not allow him to challenge the terms of the debate or to undo the either/or logic of this debate's underlying question—namely, whether sex is good or bad. Ultimately, a critique of the religious right's attack on gay male sexuality can never be effective if it is couched in the same rhetoric as is that attack. On the contrary, we need to queer the rhetorical strategies we employ to move beyond the distracting question of whether gay promiscuity is good or bad.

3

How Gay Theory and the Gay Movement
Betrayed the Sissy Boy

Portrait of the Author as a Young Fag?

Looking at some photographs of me as a young child, a friend exclaimed: "Boy, you were such a little faggot, how could your parents not know you were gay?" Instead of being offended by my friend's bluntness, I appreciated his unequivocal statement of something I had always felt but had never been able to put into words—I have always been that way, even before I knew what "that way" meant. The surprising thing, of course, is that the pictures we pored over were taken when I was five or six, long before I knew what homosexuality was, long before I had sex with a man or another boy, and definitely long before I came to think of myself as being homosexual, let alone gay. What does it mean to say that I can see my gayness in photographs of me as a child? What knowledge, present now but absent then, makes possible this retrospective assignment of meaning to a visual representation of myself as a young boy? Has my homosexuality always been written on my body?

One way that homosexuality *has* historically been written on the body, of course, is through its expression of so-called abnormal gender characteristics. Thus, the concept of "inversion," which goes back at least to the nineteenth century and provided a popular term for homosexuality up to the 1950s, posited a display of attributes of the "opposite sex" as symptomatic of abnormal sexual desires. Sexologists such as Karl Heinrich Ulrichs, Richard von Krafft-Ebing, and Havelock Ellis explained homosexuality as a congenital abnormality that results from a mismatch between physiological sex and emotional gender: homosexual men are female "souls" trapped in male bodies; lesbians are male "souls" trapped in women's bodies. Conceptualizing homosexuality as a naturally occurring abnormality rather than a moral failing (as it was previously thought to be) allowed those who claimed the invert label to argue that they were unable to do anything about their sexuality and therefore should not be prosecuted. In this respect, the sexologists' theory of inversion lent itself to a progressive homosexual politics at the beginning of the twentieth century. Unfortunately, this early explanation of congenital homosexuality also resulted in the creation of stereotypes for the congenitally inverted woman and man: the mannish lesbian and the effeminate homosexual man, with images of the "disease of effeminacy" in males dominating the popular imagination.

While the homophile movement accepted the dominant psychiatric conception of homosexuality as a congenital disorder, frequently seeking the opinion of (mostly medical) "experts" on the "homosexual condition," gay liberation was unequivocal in its opposition to such expert opinions, arguing that the classification and treatment of homosexuality as a pathology fostered the oppression of gays and lesbians. Beginning in the 1970s, individuals working in gay theory and the gay movement argued that homosexuality should be theorized independently of cross-gender behavior and pointed out that neither excessive femininity in males nor excessive masculinity in females is a prerequisite for homosexual desire. Whereas the theory of congenital inversion functioned as a means for positing, by contradistinction, what constitutes proper masculinity in men and proper femininity in women, gay liberationists championed the idea that "one woman, *as a woman,* might desire another; that one man, *as a man,* might desire another."[1] This theoretical and political shift manifested itself most visibly in the gay male culture of the 1970s and early 1980s as gay men en masse reacted to the stereotype of the effeminate homosexual by fashioning the "clone" look, which promoted the display of explicit masculinity: short hair; beards, mustaches, and sideburns; and tight-fitting jeans to emphasize the buttocks and the crotch.[2]

In this chapter I argue that precisely this preoccupation with the image of the masculine gay man left gay theory and gay politics ill-equipped to intervene in the "war against effeminate boys,"[3] inaugurated in 1980 by the American Psychiatric Association's creation of a new category within the third edition of its *Diagnostic and Statistical Manual:* gender identity disorder (GID) of childhood. This new and problematic diagnostic category, introduced a mere seven years after the APA's groundbreaking decision to drop the pathologizing diagnosis of homosexuality from its manual, made possible the diagnosis and treatment of cross-gendered children as "prehomosexual." In fact, the *DSM-III,* the first edition of the manual that does not contain an entry for homosexuality, is also the first that does contain an entry for GID.[4] Psychiatry's vilification of gender-queer behavior in children amounts to a renewed pathologizing of homosexuality. Gay theory and the gay movement have betrayed the sissy boy by not speaking out against psychiatry's introduction of this new diagnosis.

On Being "Disordered"

In 1970 gay and lesbian activists began interrupting the annual meetings of the American Medical Association and the American Psychiatric Association to protest the continued pathologizing of homosexuality. For example, in *A Leaflet for the American Medical Association* the Chicago Gay Liberation Front rejected what it called the "adjustment school" of psychiatry. This approach, the group argued, "places the burden on each homosexual individual to learn to bear his torment. But the 'problem' of homosexuality is never solved under this scheme; the anti-homosexualist attitude of society, which is the cause of the homosexual's trouble, goes unchallenged."[5] This kind of argumentation also lies at the heart of a film by the German director Rosa von Praunheim that was released the same year as the leaflet. The title of Praunheim's film sums up the homosexual subject's situation quite pointedly: *Nicht der Homosexuelle ist pervers, sondern die Situation, in der er lebt* (released in the United States in 1971 under a title close to the German one: *It Is Not the Homosexual Who Is Perverted, but the Society in Which He Lives*).

The gay and lesbian campaigns were successful. In 1973 the American Psychiatric Association voted to remove homosexuality from the list of psychiatric disorders in its *Diagnostic and Statistical Manual.* Today only a small fringe group of professionals still holds on to the concept of "reparative therapy," at times even resorting to aversion therapy, whose hoped-for outcome is the patient's conversion from homo- to heterosexuality.[6] The majority of experts in the field, however, appear to be more enlightened. They no longer attempt to "cure" homosexuals; rather, they help them claim a sexual identity that can serve their clients as armor, protecting them from homophobic attacks in a heterosexist society. After all, it takes considerable strength to declare that you are gay—let alone that "gay is good"—in a culture that continually casts homosexuality as unnatural, sinful, inferior to heterosexuality, or just plain wrong.[7]

Nonetheless, as I mentioned earlier, the *DSM-III* was also the first edition of the manual to include the new diagnostic category of gender identity disorder of childhood. As Matthew Rottnek explains, "with the diagnosis of Gender Identity Disorder (GID), cross-gendered behavior or cross-gendered identification in children—for example, cross-dressing, playing with toys traditionally associated with the opposite sex, a desire to be of the opposite sex, or a belief that one is of or will become the opposite sex—if sufficiently rigid and if accompanied by sufficient psychic stress, may be deemed an illness."[8] The literature on cross-gender identification that developed in the wake of this new diagnosis focused almost exclusively on boys, with Richard's Green's book *The "Sissy Boy Syndrome" and the Development of Homosexuality* being perhaps the best-known example. In this longitudinal study of male homosexual behavior from early childhood to young adulthood, Green claims that there is a "linkage between boyhood 'femininity' and manhood homosexuality."[9] In other words, cross-gendered boys (are likely to) grow up to be homosexual men. Green also speaks of the "powerlessness of treatment to interrupt the progression from 'feminine' boy to homosexual man."[10]

Unfortunately, Green's declaration has not stopped some psychiatrists who to this day consider homosexuality a disorder in need of treatment. These doctors continue to make the most of the diagnosis of childhood GID in their crusade against homosexuality. Thus, Charles Socarides, a prominent New York psychoanalyst who is the cofounder and a past president of the National Association for Research and Treatment of Homosexuality (NARTH), sees the diagnosis of GID as a means to identify and treat "prehomosexual" children and thus prevent adult homosexuality. NARTH, a national association of mental-health professionals, most of whom have been discredited or disbarred by their professional organizations (the American Psychiatric Association and the American Psychological Association), views its mission as providing "psychological understanding of the cause, treatment and behavior patterns associated with homosexuality."[11] To this end, the group has set up an international referral service listing licensed therapists offering sexual reorientation treatment in the United States, Canada, Europe, and Australia and distributes literature to college, high school, and community libraries; the texts include NARTH's own pamphlet *Homosexual Advocacy Groups and Your School,* sent to every U.S. school superintendent.[12]

The connection NARTH sees between cross-gendered children and adult homosexuals becomes apparent through the juxtaposition of two paragraphs from its statement of purpose, published on the organization's Web site. On the one hand, NARTH laments that "gender-disturbed children are no longer helped to become more comfortable with their own biological sex, or with the same-sex peers they have been avoiding. Instead, counselors tell their parents, 'Your child is fine—the only problem is with society.'"[13] As can be attested by countless children whose parents have forced them into psychological or psychiatric treatment to change their cross-gender behavior, the image of tolerant, noninterventionist "counselors" conjured here bears no resemblance to the experience of gender-nonconforming children within the mental-health system. A subsequent statement about the dangers of homosexuality shows why NARTH puts a premium on being comfortable with one's "own biological sex" and same-sex peers: "Homosexuality distorts the natural bond of friendship that would naturally unite persons of the same sex. It threatens the continuity of traditional male-female marriage—a bond which is naturally anchored by the complementarity of the sexes, and has long been considered essential for the protection of children."[14]

NARTH adherents believe that being comfortable with one's own sex means engaging in gender-appropriate play with same-sex peers and that by tolerating violations of these iron-clad rules, parents and counselors foster the development of homosexual teens and adults. These young homosexuals ignore the supposed fact that man and woman naturally complement each other, and they thus become unsuitable for marriage, the bond that is intended to join the two. Because sissies and tomboys grow up to be homosexuals who disrupt the order of things unless concerned mental-health professionals intervene in time, NARTH recommends enforcing gender conformity at an early age as the most effective way of preventing adult homosexuality. According to the NARTH philosophy, intervention at a later date is possible, albeit considerably more difficult, by promoting "teen awareness that homosexual attractions do not necessarily make one a homosexual." Reparative theory is imperative, according to NARTH, because "many a teen goes through temporary episodes of idealization of same-sex peers; led to believe he is gay, such a young person may later find himself trapped in an unwanted—and even life threatening—sexual habit pattern."[15] Thus construed, reparative therapy becomes a benevolent if not lifesaving enterprise.

Similarly, George Rekers, of the University of South Carolina and the explicitly antigay Family Research Council, sees GID as a prehomosexual stage, the timely treatment of which may "prevent severe sexual problems of adulthood such as [. . .] homosexuality [. . .] that are highly resistant to treatment in later phases of development."[16] As Rottnek points out, in Rekers's hypothesis "homosexuality-as-pathology is simply reconfigured as a childhood disorder."[17] This is an extreme position, to be sure, and hardly representative of the post-1973 "new psychiatry of gay acceptance."[18] Not surprisingly, many mainstream therapists have distanced themselves from Rekers and Socarides.

Surprisingly and ironically, however, even Richard Green, who has declared that nothing a therapist does can modify sexual orientation, insists that "parents have the legal right to seek treatment to modify their child's cross-gender behavior to standard boy and girl behavior *even if their only motivation is to prevent homosexuality.*"[19] As Shannon Mintner remarks in an article on the diagnosis and treatment of GID in children, "it is difficult to reconcile attempts to prevent homosexuality with the removal of homosexuality as a psychiatric disorder."[20] Sedgwick goes one step further when she declares that the therapeutic strategies employed to "cure" GID betray the therapists' "desire for a nongay outcome"[21]—whether this desire be explicit (as it is in Socarides and Rekers) or disavowed (as it is in Green). Instead of being gay affirming, the new psychiatry of gay acceptance turns out to be an expression of what Sedgwick calls the "hygienic Western fantasy of a world without any more homosexuals in it."[22] Recommending itself as a practical means to turn this bizarre fantasy into reality, revisionist psychiatry seems far from actually accepting gay people; rather, it comes across as an early intervention program designed to nip the "problem" of homosexuality in the bud.

On Being Well Adjusted

Although the decision to remove homosexuality from the list of psychological disorders was a controversial and public one, the addition of childhood GID attracted virtually no attention outside the mental-health profession for almost two decades. Why did gay theory and the gay movement not intervene in what turned out to be an early intervention program designed to prevent adult homosexuality? Where were the gay activists who had interrupted the annual meetings of the American Psychiatric Association to demand that homosexuality be depathologized? According to several historical and sociological accounts of the time, they were busy cultivating a new gay identity and a new gay culture built on the very gender differences that lay at the heart of the new diagnostic category.

The sociologist Martin P. Levine explains that during the 1970s and early 1980s, "gay men confronted, challenged and transformed existing stereotypes about male homosexuality" and examines the ways in which "gender—masculinity—became one of the chief currencies of that transformation."[23] In an effort to throw off the social stigma of being sissies or failed men,[24] Levine explains, gay men enacted a hypermasculine sexuality to prove that, "contrary to all psychoanalytic predictions, gay men were as much 'real men'—and saw themselves as such—as were heterosexual men."[25] In fact, the new aesthetic that gay men created appealed to an ideal of traditional (working-class) masculinity with such a vengeance that "the clone was, in many ways, the manliest of men. He had a gym-defined body; after hours of rigorous body building, his physique rippled with bulging muscles, looking more like [those of] competitive body builders than [of] hairdressers or florists. He wore blue collar garb—flannel shirts over muscle T-shirts, Levi 501s over work boots, bomber jackets over hooded sweatshirts. He kept his hair short and had a thick mustache or closely cropped beard."[26] Importantly, the clone look was not an attempt at passing, for while it emulated a heterosexually defined white, working-class masculinity, it became exaggerated into a specifically gay "hypermasculinity"—typified, for example, by the supermacho image of the disco group the Village People—that was readily distinguishable from both the working-class masculinity on which it modeled itself as well as more mundane middle-class forms of heterosexual masculinity. Today it may seem surprising that for years the Village People were able to deny the gay identification of the eponymous subject of their song "Macho Man." Nonetheless, astute cultural observers recognized this exaggeration of the traditional masculine stereotype for what it was: a homosexual style, a new way of being gay. Thus the singer-songwriter Joe Jackson wryly observed in a 1982 song that "all the gays are macho now / Can't you see the leather shine?"[27] The clone, then, was not trying to pass for straight. On the contrary, he combined exaggerated elements of traditional (that is, working-class, heterosexual) masculinity to fashion a new kind of gay masculinity that signaled his sexual interest in men.

Adherence to the clone aesthetic was frequently a matter less of choice than of maintaining one's sexual attractiveness. Thus, Craig, a forty-three-year-old New Yorker, recalls: "I got back from India in 1974, having been gone a couple of years. I was twenty-one, and I had long hair and a full beard, and I couldn't get laid. People told me I was cute but that I'd better shave and get a haircut. Everyone looked like the Marlboro Man. You had to look like a straight macho guy—with a mustache, work boots, and plaid shirts."[28] As Craig's experience demonstrates, the dominant gender style for desirable sexual partners narrowed significantly during the 1970s. At the time I considered this anything but a problem. During my own clone period, which predictably began after my first trip to the United States, in 1978, conforming to a rigid ideal merely seemed to make being gay easy and affordable—the latter being particularly important to me as a student on a budget as tight as my 501s. At the time my wardrobe was essentially limited to two pairs of button-fly Levi's jeans, a pair of black leather boots, a black leather jacket, a gray hooded sweatshirt, a green bomber jacket, a whole stack of white crew-neck T-shirts, and a collection of plaid flannel shirts. Getting dressed to go out was a breeze; basically, the only decision I had to make was which flannel shirt to wear.

What did not occur to me then was that, as Levine contends, the strict "conformity to specific normative codes about the enactment of masculinity" was fraught with problems.[29] Levine argues that "the ideals of masculinity, the homophobia, the sexism that are attendant upon traditional masculinity were all, in different doses, ingested by gay men in their development and articulated by them as they elaborated their sexual styles."[30] Levine's point is well taken. These attempts to prove that gay men are as masculine as straight men now reveal themselves as nothing but a relentless repudiation of femininity. Even today, the personals in gay magazines and newspapers illustrate the extent to which some gay men have internalized homophobia and demonized femininity. Ads in which gay men say they are looking for "straight-acting and -appearing" partners while flatly dismissing those whom they label "fats and fems" frequently dominate the personals sections of gay publications and Internet sites.

Along similar lines, the new psychiatry of gay acceptance has since the 1980s considered a gay man who expresses traditionally masculine traits to have an integrated and well-adjusted personality. Mental health is still usually measured according to gay men's successful masculine socialization and their similarity to heterosexual men. By positing that only homosexual *men* (i.e., adults) who act masculine can be "healthy homosexuals," revisionist psychiatric theory makes gay acceptance dependent on age and gender performance. Consequently, the so-called psychiatry of gay acceptance not only relegates conventionally effeminate adult gay men to a marginal and stigmatized position but also negates any continuity between the gender-nonconforming child and the gay adult, between the sissy boy and the macho gay man. This separation is highly dubious, since, as Sedgwick has pointed out, "for any given adult gay man, wherever he may be at present on a scale of self-perceived or socially ascribed masculinity (ranging from extremely masculine to extremely feminine), the likelihood is disproportionately high that he will have a childhood history of self-perceived effeminacy, femininity, or nonmasculinity."[31]

Thus, it appears that for a gay man to attain a mental-health certification of being well adjusted, with an integrated personality, he is obliged to deny his childhood experience of being different. This requirement in turn creates a paradoxical situation for gay men, in which dissociation (that is, shedding parts of the potentially integrated self), a phenomenon that psychiatric theory says *prevents* healthy ego development, becomes a *prerequisite* for integration. In other words, a gay man must be sick (or more accurately make himself sick) to be considered well adjusted by many mental-health professionals. The effeminate boy becomes what Sedgwick calls "the abject that haunts revisionist psychoanalysis,"[32] for the loss of childhood experiences becomes the price gay men have to pay for the *de*certification of homosexuality as a mental illness.

Why have gay theory and the gay movement not contested this highly contingent acceptance of adult male homosexuality? To address this question we need to return to the stigmatization of same-sex desire as a form of gender deviance. Recall that male homosexuals had since the end of the nineteenth century been described as "inverts," failed men who quite literally were women on the inside. As Tony Diaman argued in 1970, "the straight world has told us that if we are not masculine we are homosexual, that to be homosexual is not to be masculine. [. . .] One of the things we must do is redefine ourselves as homosexuals."[33] The gay movement's desire to strip same-sex love of its pathologizing association with gender deviance created gay theory's conceptual need to posit gender and sexuality as distinct though mutually implicated categories. In a way, gay thought provided the theoretical underpinning for something to which the clone was already attesting on a practical level: that "real" (that is, masculine) men could be homosexual, that "real" men could desire men. Commenting on this strategic change, Dennis Altman argued in 1982, "Our biggest failure was an inability to foresee the extent to which [. . .] a new gay culture/identity would emerge that would build on existing male/female differences."[34]

This theoretical position also allowed the new psychiatry of gay acceptance to *de*pathologize atypical object choice while at the same time *re*pathologizing atypical gender behavior. The theoretical separation of gender and sexuality has undoubtedly helped promote the struggle for civil rights based on the premise that "gay is good." Because "gay is good" only with the proviso that "gay is masculine," however, this progress has been gained at great cost not only to effeminate boys but also to adult gay men. Gay men may have developed an armor of muscles to shield themselves from the hurt of having been called sissies when growing up, but this should not blind us to the reality that "buried deep in our bodies is the shrapnel of memory dripping a poison called shame."[35] In the name of civil rights, gay thought has made it virtually impossible to acknowledge this shame, let alone address it. Instead, to effect social change, many gay men have felt obligated to renounce parts of themselves and their history by denying the fact that effeminate boys can and do grow up to be gay men.[36]

On Being Pretty

A boy's longing to dress in female attire and adults' reactions to boys who act on this desire reveal much about cultural anxieties concerning gender and sexuality. In this section I focus on two texts, from different cultures, that center on scenes of cross-dressing, doing so to propose a queer antidote to the betrayal of the sissy boy by gay theory and the gay movement. In fact, I argue that the sissy is a queer border dweller who points toward alternatives to the binary thinking that has structured gay thought.

In Richard McCann's short story "My Mother's Clothes: The School of Beauty and Shame," the nameless narrator/protagonist and his best friend, Denny, secretly explore his mother's dresser and closet. Together they dress up, accessorize, and admire their reflections in the mirror in search of a beauty that is not available to them in their mundane, everyday lives as boys. As the narrator explains, "because beauty was defined as 'feminine,' and therefore as 'other,' it became hopelessly confused with my mother."[37] The protagonist realizes that the enjoyment he derives from his mother's clothes is illicit and represents a transgression that can get him and his friend into trouble with parental authorities: "The world halved with a cleaver: 'masculine,' 'feminine.' [. . .] In these ways was beauty, already confused with the 'feminine,' also confused with shame, for all these longings were secret, and to control me all my brother had to do was to threaten to expose that Denny and I were dressing ourselves in my mother's clothes."[38] This knowledge structures his relationship to his mother, whom, he says, "I adored and who, in adoring, I ran from, knowing it 'wrong' for a son to wish to be like his mother." Likewise, the boy's mother alternately draws him close and sends him away, because she holds "the fear common to that era, the fear that by loving a son too intensely she would render him unfit—"Momma's boy,' 'tied to apron strings.'"[39] The narrator's parents eventually decide that their son needs to spend more time with his father. He tolerates his father's misguided attempts to recruit him into more masculine pastimes such as basketball and football, stating, "It was my job, I felt, to reassure him that I was the son he imagined me to be."[40] In the meantime, however, he continues his clandestine cross-dressing with Denny.

Of particular interest here is the fact that the character's fascination with all things feminine does not amount to the kind of gender dysphoria for which children diagnosed with GID are supposedly treated. That is, his cross-dressing does not involve a denial of his masculinity or express his desire to be female. As he explains, "No matter how elaborate my costume, I made no effort to camouflage my crew cut or my male body."[41] McCann thus manages to depict the experience that the New York psychotherapist Ken Corbett associates with "homosexual boyhood." Corbett maintains that in the canon of psychological literature, "the existence of homosexual boys has until now either been silenced or stigmatized. Bullies identify sissies. Psychiatrists identify sissy-boy syndromes. There has been virtually no effort to speak of the boyhood experience of homosexuals other than to characterize their youth as a disordered and/or nonconforming realm from which it is hoped they will break free."[42] The sissy boy discourse, according to Corbett, has produced a theory that not only sees adult homosexuality as the result of a pathological gendered past but also frequently mistakes homosexual boyhood for GID.

To explore homosexual boyhood in a nonpathologizing framework and "parodically [reclaim] oppressive signifiers," Corbett suggests adding *girlyboy* to the queer nomenclature. The "oxymoronic coupling of girl and boy in 'girlyboy,'" Corbett explains, captures not only what he calls "the category problem" but also "the possibility that there may be forms of gender within homosexuality that contradict and move beyond conventional categories of masculinity and femininity."[43] We get a glimpse of one such new form of gender as the narrator in McCann's story observes his friend Denny cross-dressing: "He wanted, as did I, to become something he'd neither yet seen nor dreamed of, something he'd recognize the moment he saw it: himself. Yet he was constantly confounded, for no matter how much he adorned himself with scarves and jewelry, he could not understand that this was himself, as was also and at the same time the boy in overalls and Keds."[44] The narrator's experience of his friend's becoming something that cannot (yet) be named illustrates one way in which "queer people can feel unnamed within a gender matrix that is founded on certain ideals of heterosexual masculinity and femininity."[45]

In "My Mother's Clothes" McCann also explores how a youth can be at least intuitively aware of creating a new kind of gender experience; this is revealed when the narrator says that Denny and he "met like those who have murdered are said to meet," yet he quickly corrects himself by adding, "Perhaps this metaphor has outlived its meaning. Perhaps our shame derived not from having killed but from our having created."[46] Girlyboys, Corbett notes, are all about creativeness: "Girlyboys have a feeling for artifice, beauty and style. The body often becomes the avenue for this mode of aestheticism. Girlyboys dress. They dress up. They accessorize. They delight in gender's masquerade. They do not simply throw clothes on; they put clothes together in an act of presentation. They love themselves as beautiful. They want others to love them as beautiful as well."[47] Masculine and feminine are not categories that sufficiently capture the girlyboy's experience of gender. Because he wants to be neither and more than both, he has to create a category all his own. But most of all he just wants to be pretty.

We meet a different kind of boy who just wants to be pretty in Ludovic, the protagonist of Alain Berliner's feature film *Ma vie en rose* (*My Life in Pink*). Ludovic causes quite a scene when, at a party at his parents' house, his father introduces "his tribe" to their new neighbors. Berliner lovingly shows Ludo making a big entrance. He is wearing a beautiful gown and big pearl earrings, his face is made up, his lips are bright red, and his hair is cut in a fashion reminiscent of the French chanteuse Mireille Mathieu. As Ludo gracefully walks down the stairs, the child's appearance and demeanor are approved and celebrated as long as the guests are under the impression that they are meeting the neighbor's *daughter*. When, however, the daughter appears from a different direction, the stylishly dressed child is revealed to be the youngest *son*, Ludovic. The neighbors' approbation promptly changes to embarrassment and uncomfortable silence. Echoing attitudes in "My Mother's Clothes," the kind of beauty, grace, and glamour Ludovic portrays during his initial appearance is considered feminine and hence reserved for females.

When his parents confront him about embarrassing them in front of all the neighbors and his father's new boss, Ludovic responds that he just wanted to be pretty. This response may seem to recall the sentiments of the narrator in McCann's story, but the viewer soon realizes that Ludo is not a girlyboy; this protagonist is waiting for a miracle. He believes he was meant to be a little girl and trusts that God will correct this error in his given gender. Full of hope and raised on fairy tales, he believes that a supernatural force will make his dearest wish come true: to be the girl that he knows he was meant to be. He cannot make sense of the intense reactions of family, friends, and neighbors, for their characterization of him as a "bent boy" refers not to anything the boy currently is or does but rather to something that they fear he will become in the future: a homosexual. At age six Berliner's young hero has not had any sexual experience and does not really have any concept of sexuality. The child's innocence helps to explain both his amazing certainty that he will one day marry the neighbors' son and his utter lack of comprehension as to why the community might consider this to be a problem. When his mother explains that boys can't marry boys, he replies "I know," and his expression lets her know that she is stating the obvious. When Ludovic explains, "I'm a boy now, but one day I'll be a girl," it makes perfect sense to him. It's like saying, "One day I'll be a grown up." Whereas the nameless narrator in "My Mother's Clothes" does not try to hide his closely cropped hair or his male body, Ludo feels that his body is an error and hopes that his current incarnation will be only temporary. As members of the audience, we can see how much he likes to groom himself in ways that he deems appropriately feminine and how devastated he is when, in a fit of anger and despair, his mother gives him a crew cut. Berliner's Ludovic is not a girlyboy, he is a "girlboy" (une garçonfille), a boy waiting or destined to become a girl.

It would be all too easy to think of McCann's central character as a girlyboy who grows up to be a masculine gay man and therefore does not warrant the diagnosis of childhood GID and to think of the protagonist of Berliner's film as someone who does, but this has not been my purpose here. For one thing, we can't be too sure about McCann's protagonist. The narrator tells us that he grows up to be a man who stands six feet, two inches tall; is often mistaken for a former football player; and wears the "standard garb of the urban American gay man" of the 1980s—L. L. Bean khaki trousers, a Lacoste shirt, and Weejuns. Yet appearances can be deceiving, and the narrator suggests as much when he asks the reader: "Why do I tell you these things? Am I trying—not subtly—to inform us of my 'maleness,' to reassure us that I have 'survived' without noticeable 'complexes'? Or is this my urge, my constant urge, to complicate my portrait of myself to both of us, so that I might layer my selves like so many multicolored crinoline slips, each rustling as I walk? When the wind blows, lifting my skirt, I do not know which slip will be revealed."[48] What looks like a garden variety masculine gay man turns out to be a much more complicated creature after all, one for whom, even as an adult, neither a masculine nor a feminine categorization sufficiently captures the vicissitudes of gender.

McCann's nameless protagonist and Ludovic show us the psychic pain created when medical and cultural discourses restrain gender as an either/or binary that confuses conformity with health and variance with pathology. In this context, Corbett's effort to rethink the boyhood experiences of gay men in a way that does not characterize that experience as disordered or deviant is certainly helpful. By foregrounding the link between boyhood femininity and adult homosexuality, long ignored by gay theorists, he is able to challenge the narrow range of what mental-health professionals have traditionally deemed

How do we know?
Why do we want to know?
Who makes up these questions?
Where do these questions get asked?
Who gets to ask them?

Reprinted by permission of *Discourse*.

to be a normal or acceptable range of gender expression and to expose the culture's obsession with gender conformity as an anxiety about and a resistance to a protogay subjectivity. Corbett's intervention allows us to see the sort of gender nonconformity portrayed in "My Mother's Clothes" not as a disorder but as a homosexual variation of a heterosexual gender matrix.

Nonetheless, the concept of "homosexual gender" leaves boys like Ludovic out in the cold. While he, too, is depicted as what we might call "differently gendered" and suffers from a rigid gender system in which variation is erased, his experience cannot be adequately described as a homosexual boyhood. The term *queer,* however, "embraces, instead of repudiating, what have for many of us been formative childhood experiences of difference and stigmatization,"[49] yet it does this without limiting this experience of a "difference within" to the boyhood experiences of gays. In fact, Berliner's film reminds us of the need to theorize gender without merely adding "homosexual gender" to the dominant concept of heterosexual gender.

At the beginning of this chapter I asked whether one can see a person's homosexuality in his or her childhood photographs. Queer theory makes it possible to address this question, as well as the conflation of gender and sexuality such a question presupposes, in critical and political terms. I chose Patrick Wright's montage "Is This Child Gay" as the cover for a special issue of *Discourse* on queer theory that I co-edited several years ago, because I believed—and still believe—that this deceptively simple piece, combining two childhood photographs with five short questions, powerfully exemplifies a politically engaged response to the question its title poses. What I did not realize at the time was that Wright's montage could also be read as an illustration of the difference between a gay and a queer response to the question. While as a gay man I may feel obliged to answer the question in the affirmative to proclaim my pride at always having been "that way," as a queer theorist I will pause over the assumptions behind this question rather than hurry to simply state that "gay is good."

Queer recommends itself as an alternative to a gender matrix based on ideals of heterosexual and (in the case of gay theory) homosexual masculinity and femininity that would allow us to rescue not only "homosexual boys" but all sissies—no matter what their sexualities or gender identities eventually turn out to be. Sissies grow up to be transsexuals, men or women, or otherwise gendered; bisexual, homosexual, heterosexual, asexual or polymorphously perverse—and we don't have to turn our backs on a single one of them to prove that "gay is good." Queer theory has the potential to rectify gay theory and the gay movement's betrayal of the sissy boy.

4

Queer Alternatives to Men and Women

I think no question containing *either/or* deserves a
serious answer, and that includes the question of gender.

—Kate Bornstein

In her groundbreaking book *Gender Outlaw: On Men, Women, and the Rest of Us,* the transgender activist Kate Bornstein asks, "Isn't it amazing the lengths we'll go to in order to maintain the illusion that there are only two genders, and that these genders must remain separate?" To maintain the chimera of binary gender, she argues, self-appointed "gender defenders" often terrorize those whom they perceive to be gender outlaws: "This culture attacks people on the basis of being or not being correctly gendered."[1] Bornstein's book analyzes the various acts of violence gender terrorists have committed in defense of the dimorphic gender system and explores the anxieties frequently triggered by nonnormative gender presentations.

I first encountered this kind of anxious response to gender ambiguity while participating in a theater workshop during the early 1980s. During a break a male friend and I went to a corner store to get sodas and snacks; my friend was still in full drag and makeup from our rehearsal of *Salome.* The woman behind the counter rang up our purchases without looking at either of us, but when she handed the change to my friend, she suddenly seemed quite irritated. "Here you are, sir, or madam, or whatever the hell you are," she said, all but throwing the money at him. Her desire to know my friend's gender, and her considerable aggravation at the way his apparently conflicted gender presentation—"female" attire versus "male" stature and voice—thwarted her reading efforts, made a lasting impression on me.

I remembered this incident when, several years later, I read Leslie Feinberg's novel *Stone Butch Blues,* the story of Jess Goldberg, who grows up differently gendered in a working-class town in the 1950s. Jess describes her predicament as follows: "I didn't want to be different. I longed to be everything grownups wanted, so they would love me. I followed all their rules, tried my best to please. But there was something about me that made them knit their eyebrows and frown. No one ever offered a name for what was wrong with me. That's what made me afraid it was really bad. I only came to recognize its melody through this constant refrain: 'Is it a boy or a girl?'"[2] As Jess gets older, the refrain changes to "Is that a man or a woman?" but Feinberg makes it clear that people's desires to know her protagonist's gender remain as persistent as the disapproving and angry reactions Jess meets when those desires are frustrated.

Years later I was reminded of both Feinberg's novel and the incident in the grocery store when I watched an episode of the *Maury Povich Show* that once again, albeit from a different perspective and for different purposes, called into question what is at stake in (mis)reading someone's gender. This particular episode, first broadcast in 1999 and featuring nearly a dozen drag kings, not only shows how the drag king phenomenon has been made to signify in certain spheres of popular culture but also speaks volumes about the anxieties that attach to gender ambiguity and to people who do not stick to their assigned gender or whose gender cannot be readily perceived.

In the circus atmosphere of the *Maury Povich Show,* gender ambiguity becomes a guessing game with audience participation. Fourteen "contestants" are introduced to the audience by male (stage)names—Wayne, Mr. D., Tyler, Smoov Dawg, Fresh, and so on—in outfits ranging from blue-collar work clothes to tuxedos. The show's title, "I'm a Real Man . . . or Am I?" marks the featured drag kings as pretenders whom the audience is invited to distinguish from men whose own masculinities are represented as authentic, albeit ambiguous. The spectators' task, in other words, is to tell "real men" (whose appearances—their lack of height or their slight builds—enter them only partially into the norm of masculinity and implicate them as male impostors) from the "real impostors," women pretending to be men. As the host explains, he will present "women who act and dress like men, and some of them are so convincing you can't tell them apart from the real guys." While Povich taunts the studio audience ("We'll see if you can figure out who's who"), the question "Man or Woman? Can you tell?" flashes across the bottom of the TV screen, extending the challenge to the home viewers. Why this excitement about guessing a person's gender? Why this nervousness about getting it wrong?

Judith Butler addresses the cultural power of gender in an article in which she contends that gender is one of the "conditions of intelligibility [. . .] by which the human emerges, by which the human is recognized."[3] In other words, we have to be able to read someone as a gendered being to recognize his or her humanness and personhood. Grammar rules reflect this law of intelligibility: if we cannot identify someone as male or female, we must use the impersonal pronoun *it,* a designation that refers to things and thus denies humanness. Because without coherent gender we cannot think them human at all, when someone's gender is in question, so is their personhood, their humanness.

In the case of the *Maury Povich Show,* this conflict takes the shape of a game. At one point in the episode, Povich asks audience members to voice their opinions as he holds his hand over the head of each contestant. The spectators respond in chorus, shouting "It's a man; it's a man!" or "That's a woman; that's a woman!" To keep viewers from switching channels, the game's resolution is postponed until later in the show, and the promised revelations are spread out over four segments. In the meantime, the now-familiar caption "Man or Woman? Can you tell?" keeps flashing across the bottom of the screen in an effort to sustain the spectators' interest. Finally the contestants reveal their "true selves" by coming onstage wearing either a tiara or a crown to indicate their genders. The show's producers seem to have been oblivious to the irony that a tiara connotes not just a female monarch but also a drag queen and a crown refers not only to a male monarch but also to a drag king. Thus Mr. D., for example, who all but a few audience members believe is a woman, comes out still in male drag, including a beard and sideburns, but wearing a tiara. She introduces herself as "Denise" and tells Maury and the audience that she is a drag king from New York and that Mr. D. is her stage persona. Likewise, Kurt, whom the audience also believes to be female, comes onstage in male attire and reveals herself as the New York performance artist Shelley Mars by wiping off her makeup and stripping off her T-shirt to reveal a lacy bra. As the show progresses, the audience members' certainty that they can correctly identify the gender of the participants increases. Listing surefire, tell-tale signs of someone's gender, they mention bone structure, feet, Adam's apples, eyebrows, cheeks, and various other facial features. One male spectator even goes so far as to boast that he "can pick them all."

This confidence is tested, however, when the audience is confronted with Fresh, an African American contestant who comes onstage singing a Barry White song and flanked by two femmy white dancers. As was the case with Mr. D. and Kurt, most in the studio audience judge Fresh to be a woman. Following Povich's prompt, "You wanna reveal yourself, Fresh? Tiara or crown?"

Fresh at first pretends to reach for the tiara, only to pick up the crown and place it on his head. The host taunts the shocked audience, telling them, "You are all wrong!"; pointing to the overconfident male audience member, he adds, "You, too. Especially you!" Just as the man admits, "You got me," however, Fresh confesses, "Maury, I have a secret to tell. I *am* really a woman." Fresh informs the audience that she was voted San Francisco drag king of the year in 1999, to which Povich responds, "If you're that good, you oughta wear a crown." The audience rises triumphantly to give Fresh (and themselves, one assumes) a standing ovation.

The other contestants come out in tuxedos or evening gowns to indicate their "real" genders, a presentation that succeeds only partially, for some of them—Smoov Dawg (Renee) and Derrick (Yvette), for instance—look more as if they are in drag in the supposedly gender-appropriate evening attire the show has furnished for them than they did in the male outfits they wore before. Somewhat predictably perhaps, we get a mirror image of Fresh's revelation at the end of the show as Henry, an Asian contestant whom the audience believes to be a man, comes out looking quite stunning in a red velvet dress and matching high heels and sporting long hair and dangling earrings. Once again, the audience is aghast at having been duped. When Povich asks Henry his real name, he replies "Henry" and removes falsies from his bra for dramatic effect.

Thus twice during the one-hour program the audience is stunned when a contestant reveals a biological gender different from the one the audience has thought to be indicated by "his" appearance—and in both situations the confusion about sexual difference is coupled with racial difference. As audience members express their disbelief, the show's atmosphere changes drastically. What seemed to be fun and games mere moments before suddenly becomes a serious problem, because those who have deemed themselves experts in matters of gender presentation and sexual difference are confronted with their grave misidentifications, and their faces register their shock. In both instances, however, the unsettling effect of this misrecognition is undercut by the contestant revealing her or his "real" sex. Beyond merely confirming that they were right after all, this final disclosure also serves to restore the spectators' psychic equilibrium by ensuring them that, in the final analysis, one can always read a person's sex, however good a masquerade he or she puts on initially.

By the end of the show, the body is confirmed as what Annette Kuhn refers to as "the location of an absolute difference,"[4] and the audience is reassured that, although the eye/I may be fooled temporarily, in the end one can still tell a man from a woman. Cross-dressing in this instance signifies a merely temporary disjunction between clothes and body, and the restoration of proper dress to each contestant affirms the "natural" order of the sex/gender system by presenting female bodies in feminine attire and male bodies in masculine clothes.[5] Thus the show problematizes gender identity and sexual difference in a most sensationalistic manner—"Man or Woman? The answers may shock you!"—only to confirm the absoluteness of both in the end. In other words, the threat of gender confusion is acceptable as a source of speculation and titillation provided that it is sufficiently neutralized by the end of the program, assuring the audience that gender can be clearly identified after all. Far from celebrating gender ambiguity or the multiplication of genders, then, this episode of the *Maury Povich Show* instead illustrates what Deborah Britzman calls "the dominant insistence upon the stability of bodies, the body as fact, transmitting obvious information."[6] In the course of the show, audience members are enlisted as gender defenders, people who "defend the status quo of the existing gender system."[7]

It is this conviction—that the body must personify a stable meaning—that also motivated a particularly violent and gruesome act of gender terrorism: the rape and subsequent murder of the transsexual Brandon Teena by two men intent on demonstrating that he was "really" a woman. This is illustrated in the film *Boys Don't Cry,* based on Brandon Teena's life, in a scene in which the two men encounter Brandon in his customary male clothes after the authorities have revealed him as female. They scream at him, "What the fuck are you?" As Brandon escapes to the bathroom, one of the men searches for him frantically, shouting, "Where the fuck is *it?*" Because Brandon continues to live his life as a man even after being revealed as legally female, he becomes unreadable as a person and is therefore considered less than human—an "it."[8] The fact that his persecutors subsequently attempt to strip Brandon shows what Bornstein terms the commonly held "belief in the supremacy of the body in the determination of identity."[9] Brandon's lack of gender intelligibility and the men's desire to reestablish the body as an unequivocal site of sexual difference ultimately result in their brutal rape of Brandon.

The two men react in a particularly violent way because they feel duped by Brandon, for as far as they are concerned, the man with whom they bonded and with whom they chased girls turns out to be a girl himself. Nonetheless, their ready acceptance of Brandon as their "little buddy" may be due less to Brandon's powers of deception than to the fact that, as Bornstein and other gender theorists have pointed out, "in this culture, gender attribution, like gender assignment, is phallocentric. That is, one is male until perceived otherwise."[10] Furthermore, as Bornstein reminds us, gender defenders have a stake in maintaining their membership in a given gender. This is especially true in the case of heterosexual men, since the defense of the existing gender system ensures the perpetuation of "male privilege and all its social extensions."[11] In the case at hand, the men who commit the rape consider it a lesson for Brandon, a punishment to put "her" into "her" place. As James R. Keller points out, " 'Fucking' is socially constructed as a sign of mastery, both in its literal and its figurative meanings; the penis becomes the weapon that guarantees submission."[12] Therefore, the insistence on the fixity and absoluteness of sexual difference is simultaneously the insistence on the stability of the sexual and social hierarchies erected on that difference. This fact goes a long way toward explaining why some gender defenders feel "impelled or even empowered to kill to preserve the regimes of gender."[13]

To be sure, the rape and subsequent murder of Brandon Teena constitutes a particularly brutal act of gender terrorism, yet aggressive responses to the threat that gender ambiguity poses to the sexual and social order can already be observed, albeit in considerably less violent form, in the audience members of the *Maury Povich Show.* There is a thin line between situations in which gender confusion is the source of entertainment and titillation and other situations in which it becomes an excuse for violence. While the reaction to the threat of gender ambiguity is diffused and contained by the structure of the show that elicits it, it escalated in the case of the gender defenders who raped and killed Brandon Teena to annihilate someone they viewed as embodying that threat.

To cross-dress means to "challenge the identity that society has dictated, to declare that you're not quite what has been determined by powers outside of yourself."[14] While this threat to the status quo was anxiously managed and ultimately contained by the producers of the *Maury Povich Show,* it provoked a murderous wrath in the two men who raped and killed Brandon Teena. Nevertheless, such contestations of identity and gender categories may be enthusiastically embraced and even celebrated in a different context, as is demonstrated by H.I.S. Kings,[15] a group of about twenty women who performed drag shows in Columbus, Ohio, from 1996 to 2004. I read H.I.S. Kings as an encouraging example showing how queer cultural practices can provide alternatives to traditional conceptualizations of men and women, male and female.

Most writing on the drag king phenomenon has until recently focused on such centers of urban queer life as New York City and San Francisco and has considered it mainly in terms of "female masculinity."[16] Elsewhere I have argued that the exclusive focus on a few urban centers misses variations and inventions within the drag king phenomenon that have developed in other places (both in the United States and abroad), resulting in an incomplete model that cannot account for some of the drag king's most interesting varieties.[17] Here I want to challenge the limited definition of the drag king as a theatrical male impersonator. I do not mean to minimize the significance of the Columbus company's hyperbolic performances of masculinity, which exaggerate gender traits for theatrical and comic effect. These performances are remarkable for at least two reasons. On the one hand, they disprove the dictum that camp works only for outrageous performance of femininity by staging a uniquely lesbian version of camp; on the other hand, they help to make white masculinity, which heretofore has been considered all but impervious to satire, a frequent and productive object of parody. Not only do H.I.S. Kings elaborate complex and probing performances of female masculinity; in addition, they expand the repertoire to explore the construction and performance of femaleness, with often hilarious and always provocative results. The fact that they perform a variety of femininities makes their sort of kinging even more fascinating to anyone interested in the construction not just of masculinity but of gender in general.

The dazzling shift from women performing masculinity to women performing femininity is illustrated by Baby T (Donna Baladad), an Asian member of the Columbus company, who on one occasion presents himself as a suave gentleman singing about his desire to *do* as the song title "Kiss the Girl" suggests but in a different number acts on his desire to *be* the girl. In the dance that Baby T and his Caucasian partner, Reardon (Jacci Morrison), perform to the theme song from *Dirty Dancing,* Baby T's femininity is set off by Reardon's masculinity, already well established in a previous number in which he performs as a man and quite rightly declares that he's just "too sexy." Reardon's masculinity offsets Baby T's femininity and bolsters the illusion of sexual difference their number creates.

The representation of masculinity and femininity in this act, however, is complicated by several factors. For one thing, Baby T's performance queers both the character played by Jennifer Grey in the movie and her relationship with the Patrick Swayze character by making theirs an interracial affair and thus undercutting the representative character of white heterosexuality.[18] More important, perhaps, Baby T's carefully crafted femininity—the girlish pink of her dress as well as her haircut, demure facial expression, red lips, and bobby socks—is undercut by a physical marker that seems to contradict this

construction of femininity: tattoos. One of the modes of drag king performance other scholars have distinguished is "layering," a recognizably "male
role [being] layered on top of the king's own masculinity."[19] This definition
may be helpful for kings who perform only masculinity, yet it seems too
limited for an analysis of Reardon and Baby T's performance, for it does
not describe the ways in which all gendered performances—including the
performance of femininity—may be layered.

In Baby T's case, tattoos signify a more masculine kind of femininity and
thus alert us to the fact that here *femininity* is being layered on top of the
performer's own female masculinity. This becomes especially clear when
the tattoos Reardon and Baby T each sport on their upper arms lie at approximately the same height. This creates a visual parallel that suggests a
kind of similarity between the two dancers, a similarity that undercuts the
appearance of sexual difference on which the performance of heterosexuality
is based and thus calls into question the "naturalistic effects of heterosexu-
alized genders."[20] The Reardon–Baby T performance calls attention to the
ways in which "the permeable boundaries between acting and being" help
expose the artificiality of conventional gender roles.[21] Contrary to what previous commentators have argued, acts like those performed by H.I.S. Kings
demonstrate that a drag king may expose the artificiality of conventional
gender roles not only through his performance of masculinity but *just as
effectively, if not more so,* through a performance of femininity.

Judith Butler has defined gender as "the repeated stylization of the body,
a set of repeated acts within a highly rigid regulatory frame that congeal
over time to produce the appearance of substance, of a natural sort of being."[22] Gender, in other words, is not authentic; rather, it is the cumulative
effect of a series of performative acts whose repetition creates the *illusion* of
authenticity. Without that repetition there is no substance, no "there there."
Gender as such does not exist independently of the performative expression that constitutes it discursively.[23] Drag offers a useful cultural model
for deconstructing the substantive appearance of gender by emphasizing its
theatricality and thus exposing its constitutive parts. Through parodic staging, drag illuminates the elements of gender, which tend to be imperceptible
in "successful" (that is, seamless and naturalized) everyday productions of
gender. H.I.S. Kings' performances of different kinds of both femininity
and masculinity demonstrate that, as Butler puts it, "drag enacts the very
structure of impersonation by which *any gender* is assumed"[24]—including,
one might add, the performance of femininity by women.

Lustivious de la Virgion (Si'le Singleton), H.I.S. Kings' emcee

H.I.S. Kings' African American emcee extraordinaire occasionally performed as King Luster but more frequently delighted audiences as Lustivious de la Virgion. Lustivious is what one might call a "female drag queen,"
presenting a construction of femininity that is "relayed through a gay male
aesthetic."[25] Indeed, the gay male aesthetic has influenced the cultural construction of femininity, as when in a widely known joke Monica Lewinsky's
nemesis Linda Tripp is described as "looking like a badly made up drag
queen," with this characterization rejected as "an insult to drag queens everywhere." The implication here is clear: Tripp's performance of femininity
appears to be lacking when compared to the more successful performance of
the drag queen.[26] Similarly, reading the first part of the ensemble's name as
a possessive pronoun rather than an acronym characterizes the performers
as "his" kings and relates their performances of masculinity to the emcee's
performance of femininity. This in turn suggests that Lustivious is not a
woman or performing herself as a woman; she is a female drag queen, a
woman pretending to be man who is pretending to be a woman.

Lustivious drives home this point most forcefully in a number based on a
song by the musician and songwriter Prince. Lustivious performs as a drag

King Luster, Lustivious's alter ego

queen up to the point where she wipes off her feminine makeup and dabs her face with black shoe polish to suggest sideburns, a goatee, and a mustache. Just as Prince poses the all-important question "Do you want him or do you want me?" Lustivious concludes her transformation by ripping off her wig and exposing a bald head. The choice of music and the songwriter's sexually ambivalent persona already introduce the theme of gender ambiguity.[27] The question is equally ambiguous, for the assumption of a heterosexual scenario here depends entirely on the presupposition that the speaker is male and the auditor is female. The performer's application of black shoe polish, however, recalls entertainers blacking up before a performance in a minstrel show. The layering of blackface on a black face, however, problematizes the construction of race and racial identities even as it calls attention to the construction of gender and the ways in which gender performances are always inflected by race. Whereas the mutual implication of sexual difference and racial difference is never explicitly addressed in the previously discussed *Maury Povich Show* episode, H.I.S. Kings approach the issue of race and its intersection with gender head-on.

Finally, it is important to note that the removal of the wig does not produce the certainty and clarity that abandoning a disguise is supposed to provide; rather, it complicates matters even further. This indeterminacy distinguishes H.I.S. Kings' disclosure from that of the drag *queen,* who at the end of a performance frequently reveals the man underneath. This subcultural convention has been taken up in a pop-cultural context by Blake Edwards's film comedy *Victor/Victoria,* in which Julie Andrews plays Victoria, a gifted soprano who can't find work in prewar Paris until a gay friend convinces her to audition for a nightclub gig as a female impersonator. With Andrews playing a woman pretending to be a man pretending to be woman, Victor ends all his cabaret performances by ostentatiously removing his wig—a gesture greeted by the audience's expressions of disbelief and delight. As Chris Straayer has so persuasively argued, "ending 'his' female impersonation act with a double negative, Victor/Victoria collapses these generic gender conventions of short hair and removal of the wig to 'expose' her (male) disguise as real."[28] A problem, albeit a temporary one, results. This revelation causes Victor to drop out of the heterosexual economy in that he is no longer available as a suitable object of desire for King Marchand, the Chicago gangster played by James Garner. The rest of the film focuses on Marchand's attempt to reveal Victoria's true identity as a woman to legitimize his heterosexual pursuit of her. The case of Lustivious is not that simple. Her performance contests the notion of a temporarily concealed female subject that can be revealed and recuperated within the heterosexual economy. Unlike Victor/Victoria, Lustivious is not a temporary transvestite but a cross-dresser whose performance of gender is layered with her performance of queerness and race. This performance negates gender fixity and promotes sexual unfixedness.

The queering of gender categories also lies at the heart of a performance by Toe B. in which he comes onto the stage dressed in cowboy fag drag,[29] including chaps and a Stetson, and dances to the Shania Twain song "I Feel

Like a Woman," which is performed by a male voice. (H.I.S. Kings' former musical director Julia Applegate informed me that she used an electronic device to alter vocal pitch, technological legerdemain that makes it possible to let Shania Twain both sound like a man and feel like a woman.) Toe B. proceeds to strip and at one point puts on lipstick with the help of a mirror. As he takes off his hat to reveal long blond hair (a wig) and tears off his shirt to expose a rhinestone-studded bra,[30] the music changes to the original female version of the song. In the course of his presentation, Toe B. takes us from fag drag to transgender drag and finally to female drag, in the process demonstrating that there are no "direct expressive lines or causal lines between sex, gender, gender presentation, sexual practice, fantasy and sexuality."[31]

Implicitly denying the fluidity of these gender performances by Lustivious and Toe B., Judith Halberstam has defined a drag king in a surprisingly fixed way as a female "who dresses up in recognizably male costume and performs theatrically in that costume."[32] Considering the multiple ways in which H.I.S. Kings perform gender, this definition seems much too limiting. Applied to the previously described performance by Toe B., for instance, it would mean that at one point the performer stops being a drag *king* and—by way of extending Halberstam's argument—becomes a drag *queen*. The focus on female masculinity in general is too limiting, for H.I.S. Kings reveal not only the part that masculine women have played in the construction of modern masculinity but also the part that lesbians and butch women have played in the construction of femininity. By performing a range of femininities in addition to a wide variety of masculinities, H.I.S. Kings challenge the overly limited definition of the drag king as a theatrical male impersonator. H.I.S. Kings demonstrate that a drag king may expose the artificiality of conventional gender roles just as effectively by layering a female role over the king's female masculinity. By assuming female as well as male roles, these performers drive home the point that any gender is (a) drag and emphasize the idea that "gender confusion" is not only, as Kate Bornstein so eloquently puts it, "a small price to pay for social progress" but also highly entertaining.[33]

How does the playfulness that characterizes H.I.S. Kings' discourse on gender relate to the rape and murder of Brandon Teena? Does the story of Brandon Teena reveal the fantasy of the drag king performance as frivolous by demonstrating that its anticipation of a world in which gender is no longer tied to sexed bodies simply cannot survive the transfer from the stage to real life? Such an argument would come dangerously close to blaming Brandon's murder on his gender play, because it utilizes the figure of Brandon Teena to construct a jeremiad warning against the consequences of messing with gender. The crimes against Brandon Teena, however, were due not to his refusal of the gender he had been assigned but to the men who raped and murdered him out of a brutal allegiance to gender essentialism.

A first step toward queering an essentialist sexual dimorphism is to question the "commonsense" assumption that the world is naturally divided into male and female, masculine and feminine. This allows us to challenge the naturalism of sexual dimorphism and to make theoretical room for alternative perspectives. H.I.S. Kings provide one particular example of such an alternative epistemology. Judith Butler has argued that because the unity of gender depends on the constant reiteration of expressions of it, gender can be defined as an "ongoing discursive practice . . . open to intervention and resignification."[34] This opens up the possibility of "subverting and displacing those naturalized and reified notions of gender that support masculine hegemony and heterosexist power [. . .] through the mobilization, subversive confusion, and proliferation of precisely those constitutive categories that seek to keep gender in its place."[35] Although the process of reiteration cannot be stopped, it can be interrupted, and its meaning can be altered through a "subversive repetition" that reveals the self-naturalization of gender. By calling into question the categories of female and male, H.I.S. Kings introduce a third term that displays (and makes fun of) the absurdity of a supposedly stable binary gender symmetry. They expose the constructedness of gender dualism and the sexual and social order predicated on it.

Queer theory has been instrumental in questioning the received wisdom of gay and lesbian studies, including the normative relations among sex, gender, and desire—the belief that there is a sex that is expressed first through a gender and then through a sexuality. Thus, Butler has argued that the cultural matrix through which gender identity becomes intelligible "requires that certain kinds of 'identities' cannot 'exist,'" including "those in which gender does not 'follow' from sex [transsexuals and other gender queers] and those in which the practices of desire do not 'follow' from either sex or gender" (gay men, lesbians, and other sexual perverts).[36] While gay people as well as transsexuals are subjugated by the sex-gender system, gay people simultaneously have an investment in maintaining a dual-sex system "to the extent that homosexuality is based on being able to make distinctions between two sexes, albeit for the purpose of choosing the 'wrong' one."[37]

This contradiction may explain why transsexuals and cross-dressers have at best an uneasy and sometimes a threatened place both in "the gay community" and in gay thought and why transsexuals such as Brandon Teena have frequently been misread as "failed" or closeted homosexuals.[38] Queer theory, however, has demonstrated that gender is a regulatory fiction that naturalizes heterosexuality (for instance, as the logical outcome or the epitome of proper sexual identification and appropriate gender expression) and excludes those who do not achieve "mature" heterosexuality (for example, gay men and lesbians, whose sexuality has frequently been represented as a form of arrested development). Consequently, any commitment to gender identity—for example, in the gay and lesbian movement's attempts to naturalize the same-sex desire of homosexuality—works against the very legitimation of homosexual subjects that it hopes to effect while contributing to the continued oppression of transsexuals and other queer border dwellers. Rather than illustrate the dangers of playing with gender, the figure of Brandon Teena demonstrates the urgent need for queer alternatives to essentialist definitions of men and women. While neither cultural practices such as the shows produced by H.I.S. Kings nor the critical analyses of such practices by queer theorists can transform the world overnight, making it safe for queer border dwellers such as transsexuals, both kinds of interventions can at least *begin* this kind of transformation by challenging the supposedly natural link between masculinity and femininity and male and female bodies.

5

Redrawing the Map of the Gender-and-Sex Landscape: Gender, Identity, and the Performativity of Queer Sex

> Pleasure is something which passes from one
> individual to another; it is not secreted by identity.
> Pleasure has no passport, no identity.
>
> —Michel Foucault

Gay and lesbian studies and queer theory have disagreed significantly over the status of nonnormative sexual practices such as leather sex and S/M.[1] For the most part, both mainstream gay politics and gay and lesbian studies treat these "fringe sexualities" as bearing no significance to the majority of gays, evincing the attitude that the less said about them, the better. Conversely, queer theory has emphasized sexual practice as an area where social and cultural meanings are contested and negotiated.[2] Queer theorists, it seems, can't stop talking about sex. In fact, in a spectacular move that accords central significance to marginal sexual practices, queer theory focuses precisely on the so-called fringe sexual practices politely ignored or roundly condemned by the gay and lesbian mainstream, positing that such exploration is relevant not only to all gays and lesbians but to all people in general, no matter what their sexual proclivities. In this chapter I explore the widely divergent ways in which gay and lesbian studies and queer theory have approached the issue of sexual practice and analyze how queer theory has radically changed our notions of queer sex, gender, and the body.

Good Queers versus Bad Queers

In her 1984 essay "Thinking Sex: Notes for a Radical Theory of the Politics of Sexuality," Gayle Rubin argues that modern Western societies "appraise sex acts according to a hierarchical system of sexual value."[3] According to a general version of the sexual value system, good, normal, and natural sexuality is heterosexual, conjugal, monogamous, reproductive, noncommercial, coupled, relational, and domestic. Sex that violates these rules is bad, abnormal, or unnatural: "Bad sex may be homosexual, unmarried, promiscuous, non-procreative, or commercial. It may be masturbatory or take place at orgies, may be casual [. . .] and may take place in 'public,' or at least in the bushes or the baths. It may involve the use of pornography, fetish objects, sex toys, or unusual roles."[4]

Surprisingly, perhaps, the dividing line separating good sex from bad sex is not as certain as one might think. In fact, as Rubin points out, a sizable contested area lies between unconditionally positive sex and its unconditionally negative counterpart. Thus, unmarried couples living together, masturbation, and homosexuality (provided it is coupled and monogamous) are inching across the border toward respectability. At the same time, promiscuous homosexuality, sadomasochism, fetishism, and commercial sex are still considered sick, sinful, and beyond the pale.

Mirroring the debates in the culture at large, promiscuity, sadomasochism, pornography, butch/femme roles, and leather sex have been central to occasionally virulent debates in gay and lesbian communities, too. These arguments have been greatly influenced by changes in gay and lesbian politics during the late 1970s and 1980s, including the shift from a *liberationist* model of gay and lesbian identity to an *ethnic* model.[5] With gay men and lesbians redefined as legitimate quasi-ethnic minorities, those in the gay and lesbian movement began to conceive of it primarily as a civil rights movement working toward equality for these newly constituted minority groups. On its own terms, the ethnic model was successful. "By the end of the 1970s," writes Steven Seidman, "the gay and lesbian movement had achieved such a level of subcultural elaboration and general social tolerance that a politics of cultural and social mainstreaming far overshadowed [. . .] the revolutionary politics" of the beginning of the decade.[6]

This success came at a price, however, for the representation of gays and lesbians as a recognizable minority was premised on the promotion of a coherent collective gay and lesbian identity, which in turn was based on the model of ethnic identities and the assumption that all lesbians and all gay men are fundamentally alike. Because the assertion of identity always depends on the exclusion of difference, the consolidation of a unified gay and lesbian identity required the policing of that identity's boundaries, which resulted in the exclusion of any number of groups that did not fit this new "ethnic" model—the so-called fringe elements of "the gay community," including drag queens, leatherdykes, and butch-femme couples. The policing of gay identity was at times so excessive that some of those who found themselves left out characterized the 1980s as a "second McCarthy period."[7] What made this exclusion particularly distressing, of course, was the fact that this time around those doing the policing were gay men and lesbians.

Although censorship and other impediments retarded the development of a countermovement, the repressed eventually returned with a vengeance. As Annamarie Jagose points out, "those alienated from the ethnic model consolidated by gay and lesbian identity did not simply demand to be included but also critiqued the fundamental principle which had centralized that specific (although supposedly universal) identity in the first place."[8] In the 1990s sexual outlaws' challenges to the gay and lesbian mainstream received renewed impetus through their convergence with the newly emerging field of queer theory.

In *The Trouble with Normal* (1999) Michael Warner lays out a polemical argument concerning sex, politics, and the ethics of queer life. Warner contends that the repudiation of sex for its own sake, characteristic of mainstream gay politics, resulted from a desexualized identity politics: "The prevailing ideas of sexual identity being what they are, when you come out as gay or lesbian the implication is that you have the same sexuality as all the others, including those compulsives crawling from orgasm to orgasm in the parks and gutters. The queer stigma covers us all, at least in some contexts. As a consequence, people try to protect their identities by repudiating mere sex."[9] This renunciation of "mere" sex is made possible by recourse to an essential quasi-ethnic gay identity that supposedly no longer references sexual acts. Ironically, this creates a paradoxical situation in which "the homosexual essence partially desexualizes (and thereby sanitizes or domesticates) the very acts that presumably called the essence into being."[10] Consequently, the repudiation of sex makes sense only in the context of the organized gay movement's attempt to achieve straight approval and acceptance by adhering to standards of bourgeois propriety. As Warner puts it, on top of his own shame for being gay, "the dignified homosexual also feels ashamed of every queer who flaunts his sex and his faggotry, making the dignified homosexual's stigma all the more justifiable in the eyes of straights."[11] In other words, the queer who flaunts his sexuality jeopardizes the dignified homosexual's acceptance by and assimilation into straight society.

While Warner concedes that the desire to be normal—as normal as straight people—may be understandable as a response to the pathologizing of being gay, he insists that normal and pathological are not the only options: "One of the reasons why so many people have started using the word 'queer' is that it is a way of saying: 'We're not pathological, but don't think for that reason that we want to be normal.'"[12] This no doubt explains the sentiment behind a recent bumper sticker: "Normal People Worry Me." Warner goes a step further by arguing that for people who are defined by their nonnormative sexuality, the appeal to normalcy may amount to "a kind of social suicide,"[13] because it accepts without challenge the very norms that made them outlaws in the first place. Instead, Warner advocates an embrace of queer sex in all its dignified and undignified varieties as a candid challenge to the existing hierarchies of respectability. "The frank refusal to repudiate sex or the un-dignified people who have it" represents the ethos of queer culture and a viable alternative to identity politics as we know it.[14]

Because queer theory, unlike the gay and lesbian mainstream, gains nothing by proving to straight society that queers are just like them, queer analyses are free to focus on the fringe elements that have been seen as stumbling blocks to the assimilation of "decent" gays and lesbians. Importantly, however, queer theorists do not assume that sex is inherently good. Pat Califia puts it thus: "I do not believe that sex has an inherent power to transform the world. I do not believe that pleasure is always an anarchic force for good. I do not believe that we can fuck our way to freedom."[15] Queer theory, then, does not start with the assumption that sex is imbued with some essential and unchangeable meaning but instead analyzes how sexual practices *acquire* meaning and how meaning changes over time and in different contexts.

Performing Identity

According to Charles Moser and J. J. Madeson, sadomasochism can be best understood as an "erotic psychodrama based on deliberate roles of domina-tion and submission."[16] As they explain, "Dominance is the *appearance* of rule over one partner by another. The dominant partner is variously called sadist, dominant, dominatrix, top, master, or mistress. The counterpart to dominance is submission, the *appearance* of obedience to a partner. The sub-missive partner is variously called masochist, submissive, bottom, or slave."[17] This emphasis on appearances, roles, and fantasy underscores the theatricality of S/M practices and throws into sharp relief the volatility of identity.

Fantasy, then, may well be the key to understanding S/M. As Califia re-minds us, "The roles, dialogue, fetish costumes, and sexual activity are part of a drama or ritual. The participants are enhancing their sexual pleasure, not damaging or imprisoning one another. A sadomasochist is well aware that a role adopted during a scene is not appropriate during other interactions and that a fantasy is not the sum total of her being."[18] Califia's clarification is important for at least two reasons. First, it underscores the crucial difference between the world of fantasy and the "real" world, a distinction frequently ignored by critics who do not participate in sadomasochism. Califia points out to those who have been especially critical of lesbian S/M that a sexual masochist "doesn't want to be raped, battered, discriminated against in her job, or kept down by the system."[19] An individual's sexual fantasies need not entail anything about his or her life outside the carefully scripted, safe, and surprisingly egalitarian world of S/M.[20] For example, the female masochist's desire to act out a specific sexual fantasy should not be misconstrued as acquiescence to discrimination and violence against women.

Moreover, the S/M scene emphasizes the mutability of identity not just in this fantasy aspect but also through the temporary and context-specific nature of the sexual dramas it involves. Califia points out that within S/M communities masochists are known to be so obstinate and aggressive that tops "often make nervous jokes about being slaves to the whims of their bottoms." After all, Califia reminds us, "the top's pleasure is dependent on the bottom's willingness to play."[21] This fact attests to the power of the bottom; in fact, it reflects the phenomenon widely known as "topping from below."[22]

The roles that S/M participants play result from negotiations that precede the scene rather than manifest some essential and unalterable power differential. Keys, for example, have been used in the gay male leather scene since the 1960s to indicate a man's sexual preferences. According to current convention, keys on the left indicate a top; keys on the right, a bottom. Keys are used because they can easily be attached to the belt loops of jeans and just as easily moved to the other side if someone decides to switch roles. Califia refers to this key code to explain the ease with which sexual roles can be switched: "The participants select particular roles that best express their sexual needs, how they feel about their particular partners, or which outfits are clean and ready to wear. The most significant reward for being a top or a bottom is sexual pleasure. If you don't like being a top or a bottom, you switch your keys. Try doing that with your biological sex or your race or your socioeconomic status."[23] The fact that roles can be and frequently are switched underscores the malleability of the identities marked by the terms *top* and *bottom* and suggests that the slash separating the *sado-* from the *maso-* in S/M signifies a very permeable boundary indeed.

Today the roles of top and bottom are less clearly defined and even more transferable than they were in the 1960s. Thus, Califia writes, "I started exploring S/M as a bottom, and I still put my legs in the air now and then. I have never asked a submissive to do something I haven't done or couldn't do."[24] The assumption here is that knowing what it feels like to experience what one's partner is experiencing fosters respect for the partner's physical limits and thus contributes to the safety of S/M encounters. Such switching can also increase the top's ability to pleasure the bottom, since the top has literally been in the bottom's position.[25] The theater of S/M calls into question traditional definitions of identity as stable and unchanging, for how could we conceive of identity as permanent if appearances can be deceiving and roles can be assumed as easily as they can be cast off?

Fuck Your Gender

Gender has been so central to traditional conceptualizations of sexual identity that even temporary aberrations—for example, lesbians who occasionally cross the "great divide" to have sex with men—are frequently considered inexcusable transgressions that supposedly jeopardize the cohesion of the tribe, and those who commit these unspeakable acts stand accused of being traitors for sleeping with the enemy. Leather sex challenges not only this kind of gender separatism but also the organization of desire along the lines of sexual identity. What matters in S/M scenes is less the status of one's sexual partners as homo-, hetero-, or bisexual than the participants' preferences for particular sexual acts or fantasies.

As Califia suggests, in some S/M practices and scenes the gender of one's partner(s) may become all but irrelevant. She explains, "If I had a choice between being shipwrecked on a desert island with a vanilla lesbian and a hot male masochist, I'd pick the boy. This is the kind of sex I like—sex that tests physical limits within a context of polarized roles."[26] Califia's statement suggests that what really matters in S/M is the kind of sex one has, not whether one has sex with a male or a female. This is not to suggest that masculinity and femininity do not play an important part in S/M encounters. Such sexuality, however, tends to denaturalize the traditionally assumed links between masculinity and maleness and femininity and femaleness. "Our society strives to make masculinity in men and femininity in women appear natural and biologically determined. Fetish costumes violate this rule by being too theatrical and deliberate."[27] Gayle Rubin similarly argues that "there are more ways to be butch" than "there are ways for men to be masculine," since "when women appropriate masculine styles[,] the element of travesty produces new significance and meaning."[28] Undermining the notion that biology is destiny, the theatricality of S/M can suspend any causal connection between biological sex, gender performance, and sexual expression. S/M makes masculinity and femininity available to all participants, whether male or female.

The fact that some S/M practices allow participants to step outside the usually rigid boundaries of sexual orientation in turn allows them to transgress the supposedly inviolate line between gay men and lesbians. "I have sex with faggots. And I'm a lesbian," writes Califia.[29] "In a funny way," she muses elsewhere, "when two [such] people of opposite sexes make it, it's still gay sex."[30] Her use of the term *gay sex* to describe an act that involves two people of "opposite" sexes may seem jarring considering that it has traditionally been considered a synonym for same-sex erotic activities. Because the term *queer* does not necessarily focus on the gender of one's sexual object, however, it can accommodate the sexual practice to which Califia refers. In other words, a dyke and a faggot can definitely have *queer* sex.

The Dildo

The simulacrum is never that which conceals the truth—
it is the truth which conceals that there is none.
The simulacrum is true.

   —Jean Baudrillard

Dildos are measured from their bases to their heads, making allowances
for slight loss in length if they are to be used with a harness.

   —June L. Reich

There is more to the gender-bending aspect of lesbian S/M than just fetish costumes and scripted roles, for it is frequently aided by what Lynda Hart humorously describes as "playful instruments that are appreciated for their utility [and] their very ability to appear and to disappear (into a dresser drawer)."[31] We are, of course, talking about dildos. Donna Haraway has argued that the technologically extended human body can signify a range of "disturbingly and pleasurably tight coupling[s]" rendering thoroughly ambiguous the "difference between natural and artificial, mind and body," and even the "boundary between physical and non-physical."[32] Given this ambiguity, it may not be surprising that narratives and testimonials of lesbian S/M frequently feature the dildo not as prosthesis but as "the real thing." Following Jean Baudrillard, we might say that the dildo is not an imitation or a substitute but rather a simulacrum, a copy for which there is no original.[33]

As June Reich points out, "The dildo, by itself, is a funny-looking piece of molded silicone or rubber. But in context, it is a powerful fucker. It is the law of the Daddy Butch. As a phallus, it assures difference without essentializing gender."[34] The dildo's realness, then, is determined not by referencing some objective truth—for example, a penis—but by comparing it to other simulacra and evaluating its efficacy in a sexual scene. This allows a female sexual actor to "be the man" without actually becoming a man.

These theoretical distinctions may be usefully applied to a scene in Carol A. Queen's wonderfully outrageous erotic short story "The Leather Daddy and the Femme,"[35] in which the femme narrator uses a strap-on dildo to have sex with a gay leather daddy. Once everything is in place, the narrator/protagonist's perception of reality changes dramatically. On a semantic level this change manifests itself most noticeably in the frequent substitution of the terms *cock* and *dick* for what has hitherto been referred to as a dildo. The narrator comments on this conversion when she writes, "Reflexively I stroked the dildo, my cock now, feeling its heft. [...] I jacked off for a few minutes." Subsequently, she decides to surprise daddy, who is in the bathroom taking a shower: "Seeing him naked I caught my breath; seeing my cock he caught his. [...] Then he knelt to me and took the head of my cock in his lips."[36] The sex play continues, and the narrator becomes more daring, as the following passage demonstrates: "I was trusting my intuition, and right now my intuition was operating out of the head of my dick. My intuition was about to sink balls-deep into his ass. [...] I pulled him against me and my dick sank home. [...] He was the most gorgeous fucking thing I'd ever seen, a strong nasty man impaled on my cock. [...] I slammed my cock into his ass ... and through my dick felt him soar up toward orgasm."[37] The transformation that the technologically extended body undergoes in this context demonstrates that within the libidinal economy of that particular scene, there are no structural differences between a strap-on and a man. The dildo functions not just *like* a phallus but actually *as* a phallus—without, however, referencing the penis—because both partners agree that it is a phallus and because the sexual roles they assume are determined by that reality.[38]

This becomes pointedly clear when the protagonist recalls a situation in which the dildo signified quite differently, when her female ex-lover used a dildo on her in a restroom stall: "It was lavender silicone and not shaped like a cock at all. It wasn't even *meant* to be a cock, on her. She never was all that turned on to cocks, but strapping something on to fuck with, something that let her pin me to a bed or a wall, [...] *that* she liked just fine. [...] She didn't think of it as a cock so I didn't either."[39] In this scene the dildo clearly does not function as a phallus. Instead, it is described in purely utilitarian terms as something to fuck with. This suggests that how and what the dildo means depends on the context in which it is used. Thus, in her encounter with the daddy, it does become a phallus precisely because it is *meant* to be one, because both partners agree that it is a phallus and use it as such, employing it as a phallus in a number of ways, including anal intercourse.

Surprisingly, perhaps, the realness effect of a dildo functioning as a phallus is not minimized or called into question by its undeniable materiality. Although the narrator frequently refers to her "rubber dick" and the effect of saliva "glitter[ing] on the black rubber,"[40] none of these references interferes with the item's functionality or performance. A phallus is a phallus is a phallus, no matter who wields it, no matter what its color or material composition. When the femme fucks her daddy with a strap-on, dildo = dick, both conceptually *and* phenomenologically.

Remapping the Body I: Degenitalization

> Down with the Dictatorship of Sex! I am for the decentralization, regionalization of pleasures.
> —Michel Foucault

In the introduction to *Epistemology of the Closet* (1990), one of queer theory's foundational texts, Eve Kosofsky Sedgwick remarks on the astonishing fact that

> of the very many dimensions along which the genital activity of one person can be differentiated from that of another (dimensions that include preference for certain acts, certain zones or sensations, certain physical types, a certain frequency, certain symbolic investments, certain relations of age or power, a certain species, a certain number of participants, etc. etc. etc.), precisely one, the gender of object choice, emerged from the turn of the century, and has remained as *the* dimension denoted by the now ubiquitous category of "sexual orientation."[41]

Despite this well-taken critique of sexual orientation as overly limited, it is surprising that Sedgwick refers to the broad range of bodily pleasures solely as genital activity. Participants in leather or S/M subcultures, for instance, engage in a number of physical acts that are not necessarily genital and are thus likely to be excluded by Sedgwick's turn of phrase.

Gayle Rubin writes about one such *nongenital* practice, fisting, in an essay on the 1970s San Francisco sex club the Catacombs. Rubin defines fistfucking (which, she notes, is also known as "fisting" or "handballing") as "a sexual technique in which the hand and arm, rather than a penis or dildo, are used to penetrate a bodily orifice. Fisting usually refers to anal penetration, although the terms are also used for the insertion of a hand into a vagina."[42] Queer theorists have been interested in this sexual practice for a number of reasons. Michel Foucault, for example, saw fisting as a clear indication that it is possible to overcome the "traditional construction of pleasure." Foucault laments the fact that "bodily pleasure, or pleasures of the flesh, are always drinking, eating and fucking. And that seems to be the limit of the understanding of our body, our pleasures."[43] Fisting, perhaps one of the few pleasures of the flesh to be created in the twentieth century, expands and complicates this limited understanding of bodily pleasures. As David Halperin argues, "whatever else one might say about fist-fucking, there is no doubt about the fact that it *is,* historically speaking, a new pleasure. According to one expert, writing in 1983, for example, fistfucking 'may be the only sexual practice invented in the twentieth century' (or, to be more precise, it *was* the only such practice invented in the twentieth century until the fin-de-siècle discoveries of phone sex and fax sex)."[44] Even if we add cyber sex to the catalog of newly created sexual pleasures, the list remains remarkably short.

Besides its relative newness, another reason for queer theory's interest in this sexual practice is the way it detaches sexual pleasure from sexual identity. In fisting "the precise gender and sexual orientation of one's sexual partner may lose some of their importance as prerequisites of sexual excitement."[45] This constitutes a radical break with traditional conceptualizations of sexual identity, for it suggests that the gender or so-called sexual orientation of one's sexual object is of secondary importance at best and may ultimately become irrelevant altogether.

In *Epistemology of the Closet* Sedgwick argues that "the question of gender and the question of sexuality, inextricable from one another though they are in that each can be expressed only in terms of the other, are nonetheless not the same question. [. . .] In twentieth-century Western culture, gender and sexuality represent two analytic axes that may productively be imagined as being as distinct from one another as, say, gender and class, or class and race. Distinct, that is to say, no more than minimally, but nonetheless usefully."[46] The queer practice of fisting suggests that Sedgwick's demand to treat gender and sexuality as distinct but inextricable categories may not go far enough. Fisting calls into question Sedgwick's dictum that gender and sexuality cannot be separated. On the contrary, it and many aspects of S/M demonstrate that gender and sexuality can be considerably more independent from one another than she suggests.

What allows fisting to overcome the strict gender divisions that seem so important to other forms of sexual pleasure? A number of possible answers to this question can be gleaned from the following passage, in which Pat Califia addresses this question from the vantage point of her own experience of fisting men. She explains:

> First of all, in fisting the emphasis is not on the genitals. Men at handballing parties don't usually cruise each other's dicks. They cruise each other's hands and forearms. It is not unusual for fisters to go all night without a hard-on. Tops with small hands are in demand, and my glove size is a popular one. Gay men who are into handballing usually think of themselves as sexually different from other gay men. They get a lot of attitude about being sick, kinky, and excessive. Hence some of them are willing to break a gay taboo and do it with a woman.[47]

Fisting distinguishes itself from sexual intercourse by freeing bodily pleasure from exclusive localization in the genitals while eroticizing nongenital regions of the body.[48] As Judith Butler has argued, "that penis, vagina, breasts, and so forth, are *named* sexual parts is both a restriction of the erogenous body to those parts and a fragmentation of the body as a whole."[49] The practice of fisting problematizes the ways in which our bodies are culturally mapped and makes an important contribution toward a new economy of pleasure by multiplying and redistributing the body's so-called erogenous zones. Foucault makes a related point when he argues that S/M practices in general demonstrate that "we can produce pleasure with very odd things, very strange parts of our bodies, in very unusual situations, and so on."[50] In fisting, this emphasis on strange body parts means that precisely because it requires but a rectum and a forearm (and sufficient amounts of lubricant), anybody who has this kind of "equipment" can play, regardless of gender or sexual identity. Fisting thus undermines both the "idea that bodily pleasure should always come from sexual pleasure"[51] and the equally misguided notion that sexual pleasures should always be located in the genitals.

Remapping the Body II: Resignification

The realm of gender performativities can be extended not just through the use of prosthetics and the degenitalization of sex but also via the resignification of sexed bodily zones. In an autoethnographic account of lesbian

S/M culture, C. Jacob Hale explains that, "as a first approximation [. . .] leatherdyke boys are adult lesbian (dyke) females who embody a specific range of masculinities" borrowed from gay leathermen. Hale describes the interaction between a leatherdyke boy and her leatherdyke daddy as follows: "If the body part a leatherdyke daddy is fisting is that which a physician would unequivocally deem a 'vagina,' it may be resignified so that its use for erotic pleasure is consistent with male masculinity. It may become a 'hole,' 'fuckhole,' 'manhole,' 'boyhole,' 'asshole,' or 'butthole,' and a leatherdyke boy pleading, 'Please, Daddy fuck my butt!' may be asking daddy to fuck the same orifice into which a physician would insert a speculum to perform a pap smear."[52]

Clearly, the resignification of sexed bodily zones is relevant not only to those who practice S/M but to anyone interested in questions of gender and sexuality. The sexual practice described by Hale suggests that it is possible to "change our embodiments without changing our bodies, that is, to change the personal and social meanings of our sexualized bodies."[53] In other words, we may conceive of S/M as a practice that resists the traditional disciplinary formation of the gendered subject by redrawing the cultural maps of our bodies—not with the surgeon's knife but through the imagination and practices of queer sexual actors.

Redrawing the Map of the Gender-and-Sex Landscape

In an interview given in July 1978, Michel Foucault compared the terms *desire* and *pleasure* and explained his own preference for the latter as follows:

> I am advancing this term [pleasure] because it seems to me that it escapes the medical and naturalistic connotations inherent in the notion of desire. That notion has been used as a tool . . . a calibration in terms of normality: "tell me what your desire is and I will tell you who you are, whether you are normal or not, and then I can qualify or disqualify your desire . . ." The term "pleasure" on the other hand is virgin territory, almost devoid of meaning. There is no pathology of pleasure, no "abnormal" pleasure. It is an event "outside the subject" or on the edge of the subject, within something that is neither body nor soul, which is neither inside nor outside, in short a notion which is neither ascribed nor ascribable.[54]

Nonnormative sexual practices such as leather sex and S/M epitomize Foucault's distinction both by focusing on (at times unusual) pleasures rather than desire and by presenting these pleasures either as being independent of identity or as potentially shattering traditional identity categories. For instance, some S/M practices challenge the notion of biological gender as an unequivocal category on which stable identities can be built and thus call into question the concept of sexual orientation, an idea that obviously has been central to the formation of gay and lesbian studies. In much of the twentieth-century Western world, determinations of who is and who is not gay, lesbian, bi-, or heterosexual have been based on desire, that is, on the gender of those whom one chooses as sexual objects.

I previously argued that when the femme dons a dildo to fuck her daddy in the second part of Carol Queen's story "The Leather Daddy and the Femme," there is no structural difference between a man and a strap-on. I return to this scene here to suggest not that the top *is* a man but to stress that in this scene the narrator specifically informs the reader that she achieves orgasm through the "insistent, rhythmic throb of the dildo's base on [her] clit."[55] This depiction suggests that the femme wields the phallus as does a man while deriving pleasure from clitoral orgasm. In other words, she does not *become* a man but rather *performs* herself as a man—and in the process comes like a woman.[56]

Just as S/M has the potential to denaturalize the link between masculinity and male bodies (and femininity and female bodies), the S/M categories of top and bottom designate mutable and easily reversible sexual positions that have no necessary connection to traditional notions of female sexual passivity or male sexual aggressivity. Queen's story illustrates this reversibility of roles in S/M scenes through its representation of a submissive femme who transforms herself into a top who tops a top by penetrating her submissive daddy. "Fuck sex differences, fuck 'men are . . .' and 'women are . . .'" she says to herself as much as to her partner as she invites him to follow her "all over the gender-and-sex landscape."[57] Finding pleasure at the limit of subjectivity, both protagonists delight in distorting the boundaries between dominance and submission traditionally associated with masculinity and femininity while rejoicing in the blissful and productive disorientation of having their identities challenged by their desires and fantasies.

That a primary identification as a sadomasochist can cut across and undo tidy definitions of sexual orientation based on the gender of one's choice of sexual partners becomes obvious as well in fisting scenes involving a male bottom and a female top. The degenitalization of bodily pleasures apparent in fisting also results in the devirilization of masculinity, brought about by a new association between masculinity and sexual receptivity or penetrability that helps to empower a position traditionally associated with female sexuality while at the same time replacing the traditional association of masculinity with phallic aggressivity. As Califia explains, "Once you've gotten two hands up somebody's ass, you aren't likely to feel jealous of [or intimidated by] a penis. Nobody's cock is *that* big."[58] Once masculine sexual identity is no longer necessarily centered in the penis, "masculinity can [. . .] be constituted not phallocentrically but symbolically, or *performatively*."[59] Masculinity and femininity, then, refer to nonessential, performative identities *within a specific context and for a specific purpose* rather than fixed gender categories that properly express one's biological sex.

In many ways S/M calls into question the assumed correlation between biological sex, gender, and sexual identity still frequently taken for granted in gay and lesbian studies. The practices of queer leather communities resist and exceed traditional conceptualizations of gender and sexuality precisely because these practices elude any simple categorization under the terms *female, male, woman,* and *man* and thus into homosexual or heterosexual. Ultimately, the queer analysis of nonnormative sexual practices alerts us to the fact that dominant cultural categories are insufficient to theorize the multiplicity of genders and sexualities already available. Thus, a critical analysis of S/M and leather sex demonstrates that it is possible to have *bodies without orientations* and bodily pleasures that are not predicated on clear-cut sexual identities.

Conclusion

Throughout this book I have clearly revealed my sympathies for queer theory's deconstructive bent. Nonetheless, it may be expedient to employ the sign "gay and lesbian" in certain situations, even if doing so seems to contradict some of the basic tenets of queer theory.[1] Awareness of this dialectic should also guide discussions about gay and lesbian studies in the twenty-first century and its difficult and contentious relationship with queer theory. Given queer theory's definition of identity as a collection of multiple and unstable positions, for instance, one may question the disciplinary formation of gay and lesbian studies and the traditional notion of identity as coherent and unified that it has championed. Furthermore, considering that queer theory has categorized the academy among the regimes of the normal that the queer opposes, one may want to resist the institutionalization of gay and lesbian studies altogether. Taking sides in the debate over institutionalization, however, is not the only way to position oneself. I want to propose a both-and approach instead of an either/or dichotomy. More important, perhaps, considering the current political climate, it would hardly be expedient to give up on the academy as a site for social change.

In a 1991 article on gay studies, the late Thomas Yingling argues, "In an era in which the virulent hatred of lesbians and gays may still be expressed sanctimoniously on the national airwaves as well as in the House and the Senate, in an era in which much sponsorship of anti-gay-and-lesbian legislation is linked to an indifference or backlash to AIDS (and vice versa), [. . .] in this historical moment, the emergence of a strong gay and lesbian presence in the academy is crucial to those who seek some site from which to speak against the assumption of power of the political right."[2] Apart from the fact that recent antigay legislation such as the so-called Defense of Marriage Act and the proposed constitutional amendment banning same-sex marriage were fueled by election-year considerations rather than a backlash due to AIDS, the historical moment Yingling describes sounds eerily contemporary, and his warning against a facile dismissal of the academy as a place from which to work for social change still holds true today, more than a decade after he made his statement. To be sure, just because the academy has provided lesbians and gay men a forum for speaking does not mean that it is beyond criticism. Critique, however, should not be confused with a simplistic disavowal of anything academic. The history of women's studies and various identity-based ethnic studies in the academy has clearly demonstrated that institutions of higher education can be instrumental in advancing social movements.[3] I invoke this institutional history here not only to save us the trouble of reinventing the wheel but also to insist on what John Champagne calls the "necessarily complicated and contaminated place from which we attempt to articulate a critique of the relation between, say, the limits of academic disciplinarity and our own continuing work within academic disciplines."[4] Given the precarious status of gay and lesbian studies in the academy today, we should not simply denounce institutionalization as yet another form of co-optation but rather accept—warts and all—the authority afforded us by this institutionalization *and* the responsibilities that come with it. Taking these responsibilities seriously means, among other things, making the critique of current academic practices an integral part of the continued discussion about the institutialization of gay and lesbian studies.

As I have argued throughout this book, the way gay and lesbian studies has been institutionalized in the American academy leaves a lot to criticize. Here, however, I want to focus on the simplistic way in which bisexuals, transgenders, and in some cases intersexed people have supposedly been "included" in the disciplinary formation previously known as "gay and lesbian studies" simply by adding the letters *B, T,* and sometimes *I* to produce what is now frequently referred to as "GLBT studies," "GLBTI studies," or "queer studies." Contrary to what this simple modification suggests, including other differences within the purview of gay and lesbian studies requires more than just adding letters to an acronym or slightly changing the label used to mark the disciplinary formation. To make room for those heretofore excluded by a limited definition of gay and lesbian studies, we need to *make* gay and lesbian studies queer instead of merely *calling* it queer.[5]

To begin with, the mere existence of bisexuals belies the binary thinking that produces the gay-versus-straight opposition underlying the ethnic model of gay and lesbian identity as well as the traditional definition of gay and lesbian studies. Of course, the exclusive focus on hetero/homo definition tends to exclude not only bisexuals but queers of color by either ignoring racial difference altogether or playing down race (or any other category of difference, for that matter) as a minor variation on a major theme. As I have demonstrated through my discussion of nonnormative sexual practices such as S/M and fisting, the privileging of sanitized sexual identities over actual sexual practices has resulted in a normative way to be queer that marginalizes those for whom the sex one has is more important than the sex one (or one's partner) is. Along similar lines, the mere existence of transsexuals and intersexed individuals belies gay and lesbian studies' exclusive focus on sexual-object choice and the unquestioning adherence to a dimorphic sex-gender system it produces. To be sure, the relation between gender and sexuality remains central to debates in gay and lesbian studies.[6] Considering the study of sexuality more fully in relation to the study of gender should not be misunderstood merely as a gesture toward the transgendered, who have insisted on the centrality of gender as an analytical category for some time. As Riki Wilchins argues, we must look beyond the simplistic political analogy "that *gay* is to *sexual orientation* as *trans* is to *gender* and start understanding gender stereotypes as an issue for *everyone*."[7]

As a result, although we ought not abandon the liberal agenda of minority inclusion that the disciplinary formation of gay and lesbian studies represents, we should challenge the modus operandi of this institutionalization as well as its theoretical underpinnings. Asserting identity in or through gay and lesbian studies while employing queer theory to deconstruct identity may seem to be a contradiction—and it surely is. F. Scott Fitzgerald once wrote, "The test of a first-rate intelligence is the ability to hold two opposed ideas in the mind at the same time, and still retain the ability to function."[8] In the twenty-first century, however, some of us have gotten so used to living with contradictions that we do not think of the simultaneous affirmation and disavowal of identity as particularly taxing but have instead learned to accept such contradictions as an aspect of the postmodern condition. In fact, queering gay and lesbian studies—rather than simply changing it to queer studies—may well be the only way to make the contentious relation between the two paradigms productive while at the same helping to ensure that gay and lesbian studies will exist in a similarly dynamic and contentious relation with the academy at large.[9] In that case, queering gay and lesbian studies may well be a first step toward queering the academy.

Notes

Introduction

1. Queer theory has been accused of being, among other things, male centered, antifeminist, and elitist. For examples of such indictments, see Goldstein, "Queer Theory"; Jeffreys, "Queer Disappearance of Lesbians"; and Escoffier, "Inside the Ivory Closet." For analyses of these and similar accusations, see the critical introductions to queer theory by Annamarie Jagose and Nikki Sullivan.

2. "Making It Perfectly Queer" was the name of the Second National Graduate Student Conference on Lesbian, Bisexual and Gay Studies, held at the University of Illinois at Urbana-Champaign in 1992, and the title of an article by Lisa Duggan originally published in *Socialist Review* and collected in Duggan and Hunter, *Sex Wars*. Alexander Doty's 1993 book on interpreting mass culture is entitled *Making Things Perfectly Queer.*

3. As Ruth Goldman points out, "Although queer theory scholars have taken great pains to differentiate their work from lesbian and gay studies, lesbian and gay studies is now often referred to as queer studies [. . .] and both of these fields are frequently conflated with queer theory" ("Who Is That *Queer* Queer?" 169). Ironically, the point Goldman makes here is underscored by the fact that her essay appears in an anthology that participates in exactly the kind of terminological conflation she describes: Beemyn and Eliason's *Queer Studies: A Lesbian, Gay, Bisexual, and Transgender Anthology.* In their introduction to this book, Brett Beemyn and Mickey Eliason use the phrases "lesbian, gay, and bisexual studies" and "queer studies" as if they were interchangeable.

4. Halperin, *Saint Foucault,* 113; Warner, *Fear of a Queer Planet,* xxvi.

5. This is my translation of a phrase made famous by Leopold von Ranke, one of the greatest German historians of the nineteenth century. Ranke set the tone for much

of later historical writing, introducing such ideas as reliance on primary sources, an emphasis on narrative, and a commitment to writing history "wie es eigentlich gewesen." Ranke's phrase is frequently translated as "how it actually happened."

Chapter 1: Forget Stonewall

1. For representative examples of books in which the American experience is characterized by few fundamental differences and an enduring consensus, see Commager, *The American Mind* (1950); Boorstin, *The Americans* (1965); and Hofstadter, *The American Political Tradition* (1948).

2. Boswell, "Revolutions," 90.

3. An analysis of the rhetoric in which Boswell's argument is couched raises questions of a different kind, too. What, for example, is the significance of quarantining the term *political* between quotation marks when speaking of the way the experience of certain groups has been erased but not when it refers to these groups' efforts to reclaim their histories? In other words, why is the straight, white, male, middle-class habit of giving universal historical significance to an extremely partial experience only somewhat "political" (in quotation marks), while a challenge to this practice is blatantly political (without quotation marks)? In this context it is important to remember that the charge of being political (or ideological) is frequently used to disqualify diverging opinions and to delegitimize stories that challenge or contradict "official stories." Boswell's selective use of cautionary quotation marks seems to suggest that the exclusion of minorities is less political (and hence more acceptable?) than the endeavor to change the status quo of historical studies.

4. This is not to deny the significant differences between conservative definitions of consensus, which are particularly hostile to gay politics, and those versions of gay history that rely on a consensus model—at least for all gay people.

5. Joan W. Scott, for instance, argues that "written history both reflects and creates relations of power. Its standards of inclusion and exclusion, measures of importance, and rules of evaluation are not objective criteria but politically produced conventions. [. . .] There is no single standard by which we can identify 'true' historical knowledge. [. . .] Rather, there are contests, more or less conflictual, more or less explicit, about the substance, uses, and meanings of the knowledge that we call history" ("History in Crisis?" 681).

6. Bravmann is adapting an idea first introduced by Michael Warner, who in the introduction to *Fear of a Queer Planet* argues that "organizing a movement around queerness also allows it to draw on dissatisfaction with the regime of the normal in general" (xxvii). Bravmann extends Warner's definition into what he calls "regimes of the 'normal' and the 'natural'" (*Queer Fictions* ix). It is this notion of multiple regimes of the normal on which I draw in my analysis of history as one such regime.

7. Scott, "History in Crisis?" 690.

8. Bravmann, *Queer Fictions*, 85.

9. The rather odd use of the term *modern* to describe gay and lesbian politics since Stonewall is not limited to Duberman but has become common usage. Obviously, this terminology ignores developments outside the United States, including the Scientific-Humanitarian Committee, run by Dr. Magnus Hirschfeld, which worked toward the abolition of antigay laws in Germany at the close of the nineteenth century, more than fifty years before the gay rights movement took root in the United States.

10. Duberman, *Stonewall,* xv.

11. Ibid.

12. Said, *Beginnings,* 77.

13. Duberman, *Stonewall,* cover.

14. See White, *Metahistory,* esp. pp. 5–11.

15. Johnston, "Firestorm," ix.

16. Bergman, *Violet Quill,* xii.

17. Marcus, *Making History,* vii. A second edition of Marcus's book was published in 2002 under the title *Making Gay History.*

18. Weiss, *Before Stonewall,* 8.

19. D'Emilio, *Making Trouble,* 235.

20. The birth metaphor is troubling for other reasons as well. To begin with, given its almost unavoidable connotations of heterosexuality, it seems jarring in the context of a discussion of the gay movement. More specifically, the kind of delivery D'Emilio critiques in this passage elides the question of motherhood, and this sexual bias could be read as a symbolic foreshadowing of the marginalization of women in a gay movement dominated by men.

21. D'Emilio, *Sexual Politics,* 240.

22. While it took almost a decade and a half before historians attempted to correct the historical perspective, the myth of Stonewall still holds on in mainstream gay politics and in (gay) popular culture.

23. D'Emilio, *Sexual Politics,* 232–33.

24. Ibid., 233.

25. Ibid., 206, 235.

26. Said, *Beginnings,* 42.

27. Ibid., 34.

28. Ibid.

29. D'Emilio, foreword, xiii.

30. Young, "Out of the Closets," 6.

31. Jay and Young, intro. to *Out of the Closets,* ed. Jay and Young, xxxiv.

32. In an instance of history repeating itself, a similar cultural trend has been observable since the early 1990s—namely, the tendency to use *queer* as if it were simply another, more up-to-date way of saying "gay and lesbian," which seems to suggest that nomenclature is merely a matter of fashion. Elsewhere I have argued that this discursive realignment, too, is frequently construed as a generational conflict (Piontek and Kader, intro. to *Essays,* ed. Piontek and Kader, 9).

33. Young, "Out of the Closets," 24. Barbara Smith recalls the revolutionary logic of the movement in similar words: "It was simply not possible for any oppressed people, including lesbians and gay men, to achieve freedom under this system. [. . .] Nobody sane would want to be part of the established order. It was the system—white supremacist, misogynistic, capitalistic and homophobic—that had made our lives difficult to begin with. We wanted something entirely new. Our movement was called lesbian and gay *liberation,* and more than a few of us were working for a revolution" ("Where's the Revolution?" 13). For a more detailed account of the early years of gay liberation, see Teal, *The Gay Militants;* Jay and Young, eds., *Out of the Closets.*

34. D'Emilio, *Sexual Politics,* 2. Interestingly, D'Emilio adds the following speculation to this analysis: "When seen from a longer historical view, however, the comparison was intriguing since the NAACP, cautious and moderate as it may have been, has compiled over several decades a record of achievements that helped make possible the black civil rights movement of the 1950s and 1960s. Did the homophile movement play a similar role for gay men and women? Did its work perhaps prepare the ground for the victories of the 1970s?" (ibid.).

35. Duberman, *Stonewall,* 77.

36. Ibid. Harry Hay was so frustrated with the conservative takeover of the organization that he eventually resigned from Mattachine. History was to repeat itself in 1978, yet this time Hay's response was more confrontational. Dismayed by the assimilation of the gay movement, he helped found the Radical Faeries, a gay spiritual movement that rejected "heteroimitation" and sought to redefine gay identity. For a more detailed account of the role Hay played in gay liberation, see Timmons, *The Trouble with Harry Hay,* especially chaps. 8, 9, and 13.

37. Qtd. in Katz, *Gay American History,* 427.

38. Ibid.

39. Qtd. in D'Emilio, *Sexual Politics,* 153.

40. Said, *Beginnings,* 32.

41. Duberman, *Stonewall,* 202.

42. *Village Voice* reporter Lucian Truscott, qtd. in Teal, *The Gay Militants,* 17.

43. Ibid. 18. The masculinist overtones in these accounts of the riots and the events' significance seems to dovetail with the inherent sexism of 1960s radical politics and its revolutionary rhetoric, as well as with the elision of women in the mythological construction of Stonewall.

44. D'Emilio, *Making Trouble,* 245.

45. Duberman, *Stonewall,* 261.

46. Jay and Young, intro., xxxix–xl.

47. D'Emilio, *Making Trouble,* 239.

48. See Jay and Young, intro., xxiv.

49. Qtd. in Duberman, *Stonewall,* 207.

50. "Frank Urges Gays," 2.

51. Qtd. in Marcus, *Making History,* 195.

52. Ibid., 194.
53. Qtd. in Pela, "Stonewall's Eyewitnesses," 55.
54. Bravmann, *Queer Fictions,* 10.
55. Duberman, *Stonewall,* 190, 196–97.
56. D'Emilio, *Sexual Politics,* 237.
57. Duberman, *Stonewall,* xv, cover.
58. Anderson, B9.
59. See n. 5 to this book's introduction.
60. LaCapra, *History and Criticism,* 25.
61. White, "The Burden of History," 28.
62. For the conservative reaction to the new history represented by Joan W. Scott, see, for example, Himmelfarb, "Some Reflections."
63. LaCapra, *History and Criticism,* 9, 10.
64. Bravmann, *Queer Fictions,* 31.
65. Adams, 48. Another reviewer similarly misses the major point of Finch's project when he points out "several minor inaccuracies and misrepresentations" in the film's account (see Bravmann, "*Stonewall,* Silver Screen," 491). La Miranda's narrative may be inconsistent with other accounts of the riots, but that is precisely the point: Finch's film presents its particular history of the Stonewall Riots as necessarily partial and contested, because only certain parts of that history can be made visible.
66. Thomas, 12.
67. Hogan, review of *Stonewall,* 36; Adams, 48.
68. Hogan, review of *Stonewall,* 37.
69. My reading of the film differs decisively from an initial review that claims that Finch's *Stonewall* "masks crucial instabilities and ruptures in queer social, cultural, and political practices [by presenting] a succession of incompatible political styles, rather than a series of overlapping, contested, supplementary modes of organizing, confrontation, and cultural politics" (Bravman, "*Stonewall,* Silver Screen," 495.) I argue that just the opposite is the case.
70. Malinowitz, "Lesbian Studies," 265.
71. Bravmann, *Queer Fictions,* 45.
72. Ibid., 85.
73. Popular Memory Group, "Popular Memory: Theory, Politics, Method," 211.

Chapter 2: Queering the Rhetoric of the Gay Male Sex Wars

1. Seidman, *Embattled Eros,* 146.
2. Denneny, "AIDS Writing," 33.
3. For an analysis of the before-and-after model of gay history that developed around a mythologized version of Stonewall, see chapter 1.
4. This phrase is intended to evoke the feminist sex wars, which preceded the gay male sex wars and in many ways also set the terms and the tone for the confrontation

between men. Whereas the gay male sex wars have focused almost exclusively on the question of promiscuity, however, the lesbian-feminist conflict has focused on the issues of pornography, S/M, and butch/femme roles. For a comprehensive overview of the feminist debates about female sexuality, see Snitow, Stansell, and Thompson, eds., *Powers of Desire;* Vance, ed., *Pleasure and Danger;* and Duggan and Hunter, *Sex Wars.*

5. Kakutani, "AIDS Finds New Forms," B1.

6. Monette, *Borrowed Time,* 2, 25.

7. Moreover, the title of the novel's second part, "1986: Learning How to Cry," also suggests that AIDS is pedagogical, an occasion for learning or a lesson to be learned. I critique this attribution of meaning later in this chapter.

8. Clum, "And Once I Had It All," 201.

9. D. Feinberg, *Eighty-Sixed,* 318; the idea of the "zipless fuck"—in part, of effortless sex without emotional involvement or commitment—comes from Erica Jong's best-selling novel *Fear of Flying* (1973).

10. Moore, *A Matter of Life and Sex,* dust jacket.

11. Ibid.

12. Of course, many literary texts produced before the invention of penicillin warned of the evils of sex and were thus frequently utilized in campaigns against sexually transmitted diseases, which emphasized the connection between disease and sex in general.

13. Larry Kramer satirizes the exhortation to abstinence—in terms of both sex and drugs—in *Just Say No.* For instance, Kramer quips that "'Just Say No' has done for addiction what 'Have a Nice Day' did for clinical depression" (26).

14. According to statistics from the CDC's National Center for HIV, STD, and TB Prevention, through December 2002 a total of 8,894 HIV-infected men and women were classified as "recipients of blood transfusion, blood components, or tissue" (www.cdc.gov/hiv/stats.htm#exposure). Nearly all people infected with HIV through blood transfusions received those transfusions before 1985, the year HIV testing began for all donated blood (www.cdc.gov/hiv/pubs/faq/faq15.htm).

15. Except for the phrase "virtually normal," which is Sullivan's coinage, all other quoted classifications here come from Bawer, *A Place at the Table.*

16. Bawer, "Sex-Negative Me," 172.

17. Ibid., 171; Bawer's comment constitutes a dig at the sex-positive writer Frank Browning, whose first book on the role of sexuality in the making of the gay community is entitled *The Culture of Desire.*

18. Kramer, *Reports from the holocaust,* 27–28.

19. Seidman, *Embattled Eros,* 163.

20. Crimp, "How to Have Promiscuity," 270.

21. Tucker, "Well, Was It Worth It?" 129.

22. Scott Tucker reports that in the early 1980s, Patrick Buchanan, discussing the

impact of AIDS, gleefully predicted "the wholesale destruction and scattering of the 'gay communities' of America within several years" (ibid., 124).

23. Clum, "Time before the War," 649, 653.

24. Qtd. in Kramer, *Reports from the holocaust*, 18.

25. Foucault, "Friendship as a Way of Life," 206.

26. Foucault, "Technologies of the Self," 225.

27. *Cassell's Queer Companion* defines a jack-off club as a place where "a number of men will gather to masturbate themselves [the ultimate form of safe sex], usually while watching porn. Such parties became a feature of the American gay life style in the 1980s" because of the advent of AIDS and the closing down of bathhouses (132).

28. Champagne, *The Blue Lady's Hands*, 68.

29. Ibid., 20.

30. Ibid., 75.

31. Ibid., 31–32.

32. Ibid., 99.

33. Ibid., 100.

34. Ibid., 124.

35. Ibid.

36. Unlike his older lover, the narrator does not have to unlearn sexual behaviors that can put him at risk. Rather, his is a tale of unlearning what the queer filmmaker John Greyson has termed "ADS, the acquired dread of sex," the result of both his upbringing and his historical construction as a gay man coming to terms with his sexuality in the age of AIDS; see Greyson, *The ADS Epidemic*.

37. Champagne, *The Blue Lady's Hands*, 21.

38. Crimp, "How to Have Promiscuity," 253.

39. Tucker, "Well, Was It Worth It?" 125.

40. Foucault develops these ideas in *The History of Sexuality*, vol. 2: *The Use of Pleasure* (1985), and *The History of Sexuality*, vol. 3: *The Care of the Self* (1988), as well as in a number of interviews and lectures. In their introduction to *The Final Foucault*, James Bernauer and David Rasmussen argue that, while "care of the self became the title of only one of Foucault's books, it was his concern with the self, and with the problematics swirling around it, that provided the major themes for his thought from 1976 to 1984 [the year of his death]" (vii).

41. Foucault, "The Ethic of Care," 2.

42. Foucault, *History of Sexuality*, 2:8.

43. Ibid., 8–9.

44. Ibid., 9.

45. Ibid., 8. While Greek and Roman ethics were a new field of research for him, his ideas about writing as a way of changing or getting away from the self are vintage Foucault. In 1969, responding to the criticism that he was always shifting his interests

and positions, Foucault remarked in the introduction to *The Archeology of Knowledge,* "I am no doubt not the only one who writes in order to have no face. Do not ask who I am and do not ask me to remain the same: leave it to our bureaucrats and our police to see that our papers are in order. At least spare us their morality when we write" (17). Foucault rejected the related ideas that identity should be self-identical and that the interests of a writer should remain as constant as his identity. Making fun of both of these misguided notions, he told his critics: "No, no, I'm not where you are lying in wait for me, but over here, laughing at you" (ibid., 17).

46. Foucault, "Friendship," 135.

47. Ibid., 136; emphasis added.

48. Halperin, *Saint Foucault,* 79.

49. Foucault, "Friendship," 136–37.

50. Ibid., 136.

51. Bersani, *Homos,* 78. Elsewhere Bersani adds: "'Don't think,' Foucault is saying to nongays, 'that you're going to get off with a Freudian reduction of your homophobia to personal anxieties; what you're really afraid of is the threat to your privileges in the gay escape from relationships you created in order to protect that power" (ibid., 82).

52. Ibid., 82.

53. Foucault, "The Monarchy of Sex," 144.

54. Champagne, *The Blue Lady's Hands,* 11.

55. Ibid., 22.

56. Foucault, "Friendship," 137. Whereas Leo Bersani maintains that gay men "should resist being drawn into mimicking the unrelenting warfare between men and women" and instead celebrate their promiscuity ("Is the Rectum a Grave?" 218), Foucault goes one step further by urging gay men to reject the simplistic dichotomy of gay promiscuity versus straight monogamy. Michael Warner, too, argues that to cast the conflict as one between love and sex is to deny the lived experience of queers and one of queer culture's greatest contributions to modern life, that is, "the discovery that you can have both: intimacy and casualness; long-term commitment and sex with strangers; romantic love and perverse pleasure" (*The Trouble with Normal,* 73).

57. Foucault, "Friendship," 136.

58. Foucault, "Sexual Choice," 22.

59. Munson and Stelboum, eds., *Lesbian Polyamory Reader,* 5.

60. Another reason gay writers are not in the forefront of these debates is that explorations of a queer way of life such as that in Champagne's novel have frequently been misread as an unequivocal endorsement of monogamy and a sign of internalized homophobia; see Piontek, "John Champagne," esp. 68–69.

61. Muson and Stelboum, eds., *Lesbian Polyamory Reader,* 2. As the authors elaborate, "while loving several people simultaneously is the reality of most people's lives, the term polyamory usually implies sexual involvement with more than one person" (1).

62. Bergman, *Gaiety Transfigured,* 127.
63. Piontek, "Unsafe Representations," 149.
64. Elliott, "The Jeremiad," 257.
65. D'Antonio, *The Fall from Grace,* 8.
66. Ibid., 5.
67. Ibid., 6.
68. Bercovitch, *The American Jeremiad,* xi.
69. Seidman, *Embattled Eros,* 155.
70. Qtd. in Crimp, "AIDS," 8.
71. D'Antonio, *The Fall from Grace,* 6.
72. Ibid., 7.
73. Ibid.
74. Clift, "Candidates Play to Gays," 40.
75. Qtd. in Turque et al., "Gays under Fire," 36.
76. At http://home.attbi.com/ ~praisinggod/BillyGrahamMessage.html; emphasis added.
77. Allen, "Falwell's Fall from Grace," 15.
78. FitzGerald, *Cities on a Hill,* 14.
79. The jeremiad also informs the "ex-gay" movement's notion that freedom from homosexuality is possible through repentance and faith in Jesus Christ.
80. Crimp, "How to Have Promiscuity," 245.

Chapter 3: How Gay Theory and the Gay Movement Betrayed the Sissy Boy

1. Sedgwick, "How to Bring Your Kids Up Gay," 157.
2. In the 1980s many lesbians began to challenge the lesbian feminist proscriptions against women's fashion and cosmetics to explore variations of the female role. Nonetheless, the "lipstick lesbian" or "glamour dyke" never became the mass phenomenon that the clone had been a decade earlier.
3. Sedgwick, "How to Bring Your Kids Up Gay," 154.
4. *Diagnostic and Statistical Manual,* 265–66.
5. Repr. in Blasius and Phelan, eds., *We Are Everywhere,* 394–95.
6. Reparative therapy, which purports to cure homosexuality, and the so-called ex-gay ministries, which appeal to it in their efforts to justify trying to alter gay and lesbian peoples' sexual orientation, are primarily based on one singular publication, Joseph Nicolosi's *Reparative Therapy of Male Homosexuality.* Organizations such as the National Gay and Lesbian Task Force (NGLTF) and Parents, Families and Friends of Lesbians and Gays (PFLAG) have long challenged reparative therapy as a pseudoscience. The American Psychological Association has declared it unethical, and according to an article published in *Psychiatric News* for 15 January 1999, the American Psychiatric Association maintains that reparative therapy is not effective.

"It is fitting," commented APA president Rodrigo Muñoz, M.D., "that this position opposing reparative therapy has been adopted on the 25th anniversary of the removal of homosexuality as a mental disorder from the DSM. There is no scientific evidence that reparative or conversion therapy is effective in changing a person's sexual orientation." He added, "there is, however, evidence that this type of therapy can be destructive" (www.psych.org/pnews/99–01–15/therapy.html).

7. "Gay is Good" is the title of two essays, the first written by the president of the Mattachine Society of Washington (D.C.), Frank Kameny, in 1969 and the other written one year later by the gay liberationist Martha Shelley (both texts are reprinted in Blasius and Phelan, eds. *We Are Everywhere;* Shelley's essay can also be found in Jay and Young, eds., *Out of the Closets,* 31–34.) In their introduction to Shelley's essay, Blasius and Phelan explain that "although her piece shares the same title as Frank Kameny's [. . .] and only one year separates them, Martha Shelley's statement is worlds away from Kameny's. While Kameny earnestly seeks to assure his audience that gay is 'as good as' straight, Shelley instead attacks the roles and homophobia that bind heterosexual men and women" (391).

8. Rottnek, *Sissies and Tomboys,* 1.

9. Green, The *"Sissy Boy Syndrome,"* 370.

10. Ibid., 318.

11. See www.NARTH.com/menus/statement.html.

12. See www.NARTH.com/menus/reso.html, where the leaflet is advertised as follows: "This BRAND NEW, 6-page glossy pamphlet strongly advises schools to encourage students to wait until adulthood to make decisions about sexual identity. Students should also be informed that therapy exists to diminish homosexuality. This pamphlet is a 'must have' for all parents who are concerned about homosexual advocacy groups coming to their local school campus."

13. See www.narth.com/menus/statement.html.

14. Ibid.

15. Ibid.

16. Rekers, "Inadequate Sex Role Differentiation," 24.

17. Rottnek, *Sissies and Tomboys,* 1.

18. The phrase comes from Sedgwick, "How to Bring Your Kids Up Gay." Like Sedgwick, I use the term sardonically.

19. Green, "Gender Identity Disorder," 2007; emphasis added.

20. Mintner, "Diagnosis and Treatment," 13.

21. Sedgwick, "How to Bring Your Kids Up Gay," 161.

22. Ibid., 163.

23. Levine, *Gay Macho,* 4–5.

24. As Jack Babuscio explains in an article first published in 1977, "Gays do not conform to sex-role expectation: we do not show appropriate interest in the opposite sex as a possible source of sexual satisfaction. We are therefore seen as something less

than 'real' men and women. This is the essence of gay stigma, our so-called 'failing'" ("Camp and the Gay Sensibility," 45).

25. Levine, *Gay Macho*, 4. Levine notes that "many of the institutions that developed in the gay male world of the 1970s and early 1980s catered to and supported this hypermasculine sexual code—from clothing stores and sexual boutiques, to bars, bathhouses, and the ubiquitous gyms" (ibid., 5). Michelangelo Signorile expands on this analysis when he argues that a "highly commercialized gay sexual culture sells a particular physical aesthetic to us and demands that we conform to it—much in the same way that the fashion, film, and beauty industries affect the average American woman" (*Life Outside*, xxv).

26. Levine, *Gay Macho*, 7.

27. Joe Jackson's song "Real Men" can be found on his album *Night and Day* (A&M Records 394 906-2, 1982).

28. Qtd. in Signorile, *Life Outside*, 53.

29. Levine, *Gay Macho*, 6.

30. Ibid., 1.

31. Sedgwick, "How to Bring Your Kids Up Gay," 158.

32. Ibid., 156.

33. Qtd. in Levine, *Gay Macho*, 10.

34. Altman, *Homosexualization of America*, 211.

35. Hughes, *Clit Notes*, 205.

36. As Sedgwick points out, the problem is not merely academic, for in this case, "the eclipse of the effeminate boy from adult gay discourse would represent more than a damaging theoretical gap; it would represent a node of annihilating homophobic, gynephobic, and pedophobic hatred internalized and made central to gay-affirmative analysis. The effeminate boy would come to function as the discrediting open secret of many politicized gay men" ("How to Bring Your Kids Up Gay," 158).

37. McCann, "My Mother's Clothes," 20.

38. Ibid., 21. Just as the narrator realizes that notions of beauty are gendered, he also intuitively understands that the definition of woman as beautiful spectacle inscribes her passivity, her role as object of an aggressive male gaze. Thus, he explains, "When I dressed in my mother's clothes, I seldom moved at all: I held myself rigid before the mirror. The kind of beauty I had seen practiced in movies and in fashion magazines was beauty attained by lacquered stasis, beauty attained by fixed poses—'ladylike stillness,' the stillness of mannequins, the stillness of models 'caught' in mid-gesture, the stillness of the passive moon around which active meteors orbited and burst" (ibid., 25).

39. Ibid., 21.

40. Ibid., 25.

41. Ibid., 26.

42. Corbett, "Homosexual Boyhood," 108.

43. Ibid., 109–10. Corbett laments the fact that it is nearly impossible "to locate a signifier for male homosexuality that does not either scapegoat women, flowers, or fruit. Consider the following list: swish, nelly, fruit, fruitcake, pussy, pansy, fluff, sissy, Nancy, Molly, and Mary Ann. Perhaps it would make more sense to rebelliously appropriate 'sissy' and repeatedly and defiantly invoke its linkage with pathology, indictment, and scorn. But 'sissy' carries implications of weakness, unbecoming delicacy, and enervation devoid of the possibilities born of resistance, agency, and action" (ibid., 109).

While I appreciate the reason Corbett gives for coining the term *girlyboy,* I still believe that the term *sissy* (or *sissy boy*) can be reclaimed in much the same way Corbett describes here, leaving intact its negative connotations while at the same time giving it implications of strength, resistance, action, and intervention. It is in this sense that I have been using *sissy* and *sissy boy* throughout this chapter.

44. McCann, "My Mother's Clothes," 22.
45. Corbett, "Homosexual Boyhood," 112.
46. McCann, "My Mother's Clothes," 28.
47. Corbett, "Homosexual Boyhood," 130.
48. McCann, "My Mother's Clothes," 27.
49. Sedgwick, "How to Bring Your Kids Up Gay," 157n8.

Chapter 4: Queer Alternatives to Men and Women

1. Bornstein, *Gender Outlaw,* 84–85, 79.
2. L. Feinberg, *Stone Butch Blues,* 13.
3. Butler, "Doing Justice to Someone," 621. Butler is here paraphrasing a point first made by Annette Kuhn in *The Power of the Image,* where Kuhn argues that "in ideology gender identity is not merely absolute: it also lies at the very heart of human subjectivity. Gender is what crucially defines us, so that an ungendered subject cannot, in this view, be human. The human being in other words, is a gendered subject. And so a fixed subjectivity and a gendered subjectivity are, in ideology, one and the same" (52).
4. Kuhn, *Power of the Image,* 57.
5. Despite the show's supposedly happy ending, maintaining the status quo of binary gender turns out to be hard work. The first problem, as I have already indicated, arises from the fact that some of the contestants look as though they might actually be in drag as they walk across the stage in clothes intended to reveal their real gender. The fact that the audience nonetheless accepts the denouement of the gender crisis that Povich offers them may tell more about their desire for a tidy resolution than about the quality of the visual evidence on which it is based. The second complication arises from the fact that in some instances the visual evidence turns out to be misleading. In the case of Mr. D., for instance, we are left with the jarring contrast between the physical appearance (male outfit, beard, and sideburns) that signifies

maleness and the voice in which Mr. D. discloses "his" femaleness. Perhaps as an effort to wipe out the memory of this queer juxtaposition, the contestant is once again brought to the stage during the final seconds of the show. "Do you remember Mr. D.?" Povich asks the audience, "She is really a she, and we wanted to bring her out just as she always is. Here she is: Denise. Denise, come on out!" Denise walks across the stage in an evening gown (provided by one of the show's sponsors), awkward, uncomfortable, and quite obviously *not* dressed "as she always is."

6. Britzman, "On Becoming a 'Little Sex Researcher,'" 63.

7. Ibid., 74.

8. Brandon's girlfriend, Lana, reacts to the question of Brandon's gender in a decidedly different way. "Leave him alone," she yells at the men. In an effort to prevent them from breaking down the bathroom door so they can ascertain Brandon's sex, Lana offers to look for herself and tell them what she finds. Once she is inside the bathroom, Brandon begins to undress, but Lana stops him: "Button up your pants. Don't show me anything. Think about it: I know you're a guy. I'm gonna tell them what they wanna hear. I'm gonna tell them what *we* know is true." To the irate heterosexual men, the body beneath the clothes is the location of an absolute difference that will tell them unequivocally whether Brandon is a man or a woman. As far as Lana is concerned, however, Brandon's body is not the ultimate signifier of his gender. She knows that Brandon sees himself as a man, and she confirms his self-identification as male by accepting him as a man.

9. Bornstein, *Gender Outlaw,* 30.

10. Ibid., 26. Bornstein adds: "According to a study done by Kessler and McKenna, one can extrapolate that it would take the presence of roughly four female cues to outweigh the presence of one male cue: one is assumed male until proven otherwise."

11. Ibid., 74.

12. Keller, *Queer (Un) Friendly Film and Television,* 109.

13. Wilchins, *Read My Lips,* 87–88.

14. Burke, *Gender Shock,* 145.

15. According to a lavishly produced program for one of their shows, the group derives its name from the initials of three founding members: Helen Harris, Ivett Domalewski, and Sue Steirer.

16. In an essay she wrote for the *The Drag King Book,* Judith Halberstam asserts that "the Drag King lives in the cities that never sleep [New York, London, San Francisco]" and "thrives on the varied queer nightlife" of these cities ("On Location," 64). Her essay falsely suggests that, since there is no "varied queer nightlife" outside these three centers of urban queer life in the United States and the United Kingdom, there are no drag kings anywhere else either (ibid.).

For an exploration of the role that drag kings have played in the development of masculinity, see Halberstam, *Female Masculinity,* particularly chap. 7, "Drag Kings: Masculinity and Performance."

17. See Piontek, "Kinging in the Heartland."

18. Jennifer Grey's claim to representativeness is already compromised by the fact that the character she plays is Jewish. The presence of an interracial couple, however, seems to complicate matters even more than the character's ethnicity does.

19. Halberstam, "Drag Kings," 260.

20. Butler, "Imitation and Gender Insubordination," 21.

21. Halberstam, "Drag Kings," 260.

22. Butler, *Gender Trouble,* 33.

23. In fact, Butler argues, "there is no gender identity behind the expression of gender; that identity is performatively constituted by the very 'expressions' that are said to be its results" (ibid., 25).

24. Ibid., 21.

25. Halberstam, "Drag Kings," 240.

26. This joke works on least two levels. On the one hand, it deconstructs the substantive appearance of gender by suggesting that femininity can be performed, to varying degrees of success, by anyone, of whatever biological gender. On the other hand, the misogynistic implication of this joke is that men simply are (or make) better women.

27. As Bette Midler says about Prince in her comedy routine *Mud Will Be Flung Tonight,* "Maybe it's just me, but when there's a sex symbol, I'd like to know the sex of the symbol."

28. Straayer, "Redressing the 'Natural.'"

29. Fag drag can be defined as performing in and parodying the uniforms of gay hypermasculinity, for instance, those of the clone and the leatherman.

30. Interestingly, the long wig that signifies femininity here can signify masculinity in a different context, as when H.I.S. King Andy (Alyson Mann) performs "Give It Away" by the Red Hot Chili Peppers, a band whose members—all men—are well known for their long hair.

31. Butler, "Imitation and Gender Insubordination," 25.

32. Halberstam, "Drag Kings," 232.

33. Bornstein made this point during a performance/public reading of *My Gender Workbook* (Columbus, Ohio, 5 Feb. 1998). As an epigraph to this book, Bornstein quotes a statement attributed to Patti Smith: "As far as I'm concerned, being any gender is a drag."

34. Butler, *Gender Trouble,* 33.

35. Ibid., 33–34.

36. Ibid., 17.

37. Califia, *Public Sex,* 179.

38. According to Riki Anne Wilchins, the transsexual activist group Transsexual Menace picketed the offices of the *Village Voice* in 1994, protesting what they described as "a salacious portrayal of murdered transsexual man Brandon Teena as a confused but sexually active butch" (*Read My Lips,* 203).

Chapter 5: Redrawing the Map of the Gender-and-Sex Landscape

1. I refer here only to the mutually consensual and mutually pleasurable form of erotic S/M. As Brame, Brame, and Jacobs point out, studies of S/M too frequently fail to distinguish between "the criminal sadist who enjoys causing desperate agony in a victim and the sexual sadist who seeks [. . .] fulfillment with an eager and consenting partner" (*Different Loving,* 100).

2. Queerness, in other words, is largely "an emphasis on the inextricability of the sexual and the political" (Bersani, *Homos,* 72).

3. Rubin, "Thinking Sex," 279.

4. Ibid., 281.

5. For a discussion of the shift from a liberationist to an ethnic model of identity in the gay and lesbian movement, see chapter 1.

6. Seidman, "Symposium," 172.

7. Nestle, "My History with Censorship," 146.

8. Jagose, *Queer Theory,* 62.

9. Warner, *The Trouble with Normal,* 30–31.

10. Bersani, *Homos,* 34.

11. Warner, *The Trouble with Normal,* 33.

12. Ibid., 59.

13. Ibid.

14. Ibid., 75.

15. Califia, *Macho Sluts,* 15.

16. Moser and Madeson, *Bound to Be Free,* 26.

17. Ibid., 30. Moser and Madeson add to these appearances four other components of S/M behavior:

> *Role-Playing:* An *exaggeration* of those sets of expectations that surround the interaction between the dominant and submissive roles chosen, such as master/slave or teacher/student.
>
> *Consensuality:* A voluntary agreement to enter into dominant/submissive "play" and to honor certain "limits." We cannot call spouse abuse SM because SM is consensual and spouse abuse is not. Just as the difference between intercourse and rape is consent, so the distinction between SM and true violence is also consent.
>
> *Sexual Context:* The presumption that the activities have a sexual meaning. SM is primarily a sexual behavior; while it need not mean orgasms or erections, it is nevertheless sexual.
>
> *Mutual Definition:* The participants must agree on the parameters of what they are doing. (31–32)

18. Califia, *Public Sex,* 168.

19. Ibid., 169.

20. Califia defines fantasy as "a realm in which we can embrace pleasures that we may have very good reasons to deny ourselves in real life" (*Macho Sluts*, 16).

21. Califia, *Public Sex*, 169.

22. *Topping from Below* is the title of a collection of erotica by Laura Reese (1995).

23. Califia, *Public Sex*, 169. Despite the lackadaisical attitude this passage suggests, these negotiations are crucial to the success of the scene and to the safety of the bottom. In these negotiations, Califia explains, the top and bottom decide "whether or not they will play, what activities are likely to occur, what activities will not occur, and about how long the scene will last. The bottom is usually given a *safe word* or *code action* she can use to stop the scene. This safe word allows the bottom to fantasize that the scene is not consensual and to protest verbally or resist physically without halting stimulation" (ibid., 168).

24. Ibid., 158.

25. Arguing along similar lines, David Halperin defines S/M as a "game in which power differentials are subordinated to the overall strategic purpose of producing human pleasure; it is not a form of domination in which human beings are subordinated to the functioning of rigidly structured power differentials" (*Saint Foucault*, 87).

26. Califia, *Public Sex*, 158.

27. Ibid., 171.

28. Rubin, "Catamites and Kings," 469.

29. Califia, *Public Sex*, 83.

30. Ibid., 185.

31. Hart, *Between the Body and the Flesh*, 99.

32. Haraway, "Cyborg Manifesto," 152–53.

33. See Baudrillard, "Simulacra and Simulation," from which I took the first epigraph to this section. As Mark Poster points out, simulacra "have no referent or ground in any 'reality' except their own." Consequently, Poster argues, a simulation "is different from a fiction or a lie in that it not only presents an absence as a presence, the imaginary as the real, it also undermines any contrast to the real, absorbing the real within itself" (Poster, intro. to Baudrillard, *Selected Writings*, 6).

34. Reich, "Genderfuck," 120.

35. In 1998 Queen published an extended version of her 1994 short story under the same title.

36. Queen, "Leather Daddy and the Femme," 154.

37. Ibid., 157–59.

38. C. Jacob Hale makes a related point in the following account of a scene between a leatherdyke daddy and her boy: "When I was a boy with my dyke daddy, in that culture of two I was a boy. I was not an adult woman playing a boy's role or playing a boy, nor was I an adult woman doing boy in some other way. Daddy's participa-

tion was necessary for me to be a boy with her. I was a boy with her by engaging in a gender performativity that made sense to both of us as a *boy's* gender performativity." Hale more theoretically discusses the idea that meaning is produced in a "culture of two" in the following passage: "I needed to know that my gender identification could be enacted legibly to at least one other person for it to be convincing enough to me that it could transform from self-identification fully contained within my fantasy structure to a self-identification with a broader social sphere of enactment" ("Leatherdyke Boys," 229).

39. Queen, "Leather Daddy and the Femme," 156.

40. Ibid., 157, 155.

41. Sedgwick, *Epistemology of the Closet,* 8.

42. Rubin, "Catacombs," 121n. The entry for *fistfuck* in *Cassells' Queer Companion* reads as follows: "Often abbreviated to just fisting. Fisting is when one partner inserts the whole hand, sometimes up to the elbow, into the anus or vagina of the other. [. . .] Also known as 'handballing' or 'shaking hands with the baby'" (88).

43. Foucault, "Sex, Power and Politics," 28.

44. Halperin, *Saint Foucault,* 92.

45. Ibid., 87.

46. Sedgwick, *Epistemology of the Closet,* 30.

47. Califia, *Public Sex,* 184.

48. Halperin makes a similar point when he argues that S/M represents a "remapping of the body's erotic sites, a redistribution of its so-called erogenous zones, a break-up of the erotic monopoly traditionally held by the genitals" (*Saint Foucault,* 88).

49. Butler, *Gender Trouble,* 114.

50. Foucault, "Sex, Power and Politics," 27–28.

51. Ibid. In the interview cited in the previous note, Foucault categorically declared that this idea is "quite wrong."

52. Hale, "Leatherdyke Boys," 230. Significantly, this process of resignification is not limited to the gendered dimensions of the sexualized body. For example, Hale explains that a "daddy may be younger than her boy, according to their birth certificates," and that "an upper middle-class professional woman can become a sixteen-year-old headbanger rockerdude with a change of clothing and attitude" (ibid., 224, 225).

53. Ibid., 230.

54. Interview with Jean Le Bitoux, qtd. in Macey, *The Lives of Michel Foucault,* 365.

55. Queen, "Leather Daddy and the Femme," 155.

56. Recent discourses by female-to-male transsexuals (FTMs) open up the possibility of yet another reading of this particular sexual encounter as a (technologically extended) female-bodied man fucking a male-bodied man; see Cromwell, *Transmen and FTMs,* esp. 130.

57. Queen, "Leather Daddy and the Femme," 158, 160.

58. Califia, *Public Sex,* 188.

59. Halperin, *Saint Foucault,* 90.

Conclusion

1. As Michael Warner puts it, "no term—even 'queer'—works equally well in all the contexts that have to be considered." As he elaborates, "queer activists are also lesbians and gays in other contexts—as for example where leverage can be gained through bourgeois propriety, or through minority-rights discourse" (*Fear of a Queer Planet,* xxviii). Eve Sedgwick goes one step further when she argues that queer theory is indebted to the gay school of thought with which it frequently finds itself at odds. Thus, Sedgwick graciously acknowledges that the "space of permission" for her own work and the "depth of the intellectual landscape in which it might have a contribution to make owe everything to the wealth of essentialist, minoritizing, and separatist gay thought also in progress" (*Epistemology of the Closet,* 13).

2. Yingling, "Sexual Preference," 185.

3. In this context, it may be helpful to recall the feminist debates about institutionalization. As early as 1987 Meaghan Morris remarked, "Institutionalization is not another word for doom, that fate always worse than death. It's an opportunity, and in many cases a necessary condition, for serious politics" ("in any event . . . ," 179). Morris's sentiment was echoed in 1992 by Jane Gallop, who pointed out that "much talk about institutionalization construes institutions as monolithic, unchanging, or even inherently evil. Institutions have histories, are in history. When we conceive of them as unchanging, we have less chance of wittingly affecting their direction" (*Around 1981,* 5). Finally, Diana Fuss warned in 1989 that "any misplaced nostalgia for or romanticization of the outside as a privileged site of radicality immediately gives us away, for in order to idealize the outside, we must already be, to some degree, comfortably entrenched on the inside. We really only have the leisure to idealize the subversive potential of the power of the marginal when our place of enunciation is quite central" (*Essentially Speaking,* 5).

4. Champagne, *Ethics of Marginality,* xxxvi.

5. This tendency to change the label rather than the content has been observable within popular culture, too. Since the early 1990s, the term *queer* has frequently been used as if it were simply another, more up-to-date way of saying "gay and lesbian," as if nomenclature were merely a matter of fashion. The notion that being queer is simply the hip, young, sexy way to be gay or lesbian has been reinforced by a trend apparent in gay and lesbian culture: using queer to market a variety of products—from popular magazines to literature, from television to independent film—formerly considered gay or lesbian. What was known as a gay and lesbian film festival just a few years ago is now more likely to be marketed as a queer event without necessarily adding anything that would justify the new label. In this particular context, the label *queer* refers to something that may be neither new nor improved.

6. A forum in a recent issue of *GLQ*, for instance, dedicates nineteen position papers to an exploration of the relation between sexuality and gender; see "Thinking Sex/Thinking Gender," 211–312).

7. Wilchins, "Time for Gender Rights," 267.

8. Fitzgerald, "The Crack-Up," 39.

9. Champagne and Tobin go so far as to define gay and lesbian studies as an "antidiscipline" they hope "will always live in a contentious relation to the academy" ("She's Right behind You," 55).

Works Cited

Adams, Thelma. Review of *Stonewall*, dir. Nigel Finch. *New York Post*, 26 July 1996, p. 48.

Allen, Dan. "Falwell's Fall from Grace." *The Advocate*, 23 Oct. 2001, p. 15.

Altman, Dennis. *The Homosexualization of America: The Americanization of the Homosexual.* New York: St. Martin's, 1982.

Anderson, John. Review of *Stonewall*, dir. Nigel Finch. *Newsday*, 26 July 1996, p. B9.

Babuscio, Jack. "Camp and the Gay Sensibility." In *Gays and Film*, edited by Richard Dyer, 40–57. London: British Film Institute, 1977.

Baudrillard, Jean. *Selected Writings.* Ed. Mark Poster. Stanford, Calif.: Stanford University Press, 1988.

———. "Simulacra and Simulations." In Baudrillard, *Selected Writings*, 166–84.

Bawer, Bruce, ed. *Beyond Queer: Challenging Gay Left Orthodoxy.* New York: Free Press, 1996.

———. *A Place at the Table: The Gay Individual in American Society.* New York: Poseidon, 1993.

———. "Sex-Negative Me." In Bawer, *Beyond Queer*, 171–73.

Beemyn, Brett, and Mickey Eliason, eds. *Queer Studies: A Lesbian, Gay, Bisexual, and Transgender Anthology.* New York: New York University Press, 1996.

Bercovitch, Sacvan. *The American Jeremiad.* Madison: University of Wisconsin Press, 1978.

Bergman, David. *Gaiety Transfigured: Gay Self-Representation in American Literature.* Madison: University of Wisconsin Press, 1991.

———, ed. *The Violet Quill Reader: The Emergence of Gay Writing after Stonewall.* New York: St. Martin's, 1994.

Berliner, Alain, dir. *Ma vie en rose.* Videocassette. Columbia/Tristar, 1999 [1997].

Bersani, Leo. *Homos.* Cambridge, Mass.: Harvard University Press, 1995.

———. "Is the Rectum a Grave?" In Crimp, *AIDS,* 197–222.

Blasius, Mark, and Shane Phelan, eds. *We Are Everywhere: A Historical Sourcebook of Gay and Lesbian Politics.* New York: Routledge, 1997.

Boorstin, Daniel. *The Americans: The National Experience.* New York: Random House, 1965.

Bornstein, Kate. *Gender Outlaw: On Men, Women, and the Rest of Us.* New York: Vintage Books, 1995.

———. Reading of *My Gender Workbook.* An Open Book, Columbus, Ohio, 5 February 1998.

Boswell, John. *Christianity, Social Tolerance, and Homosexuality: Gay People in Western Europe from the Beginning of the Christian Era to the Fourteenth Century.* Chicago: University of Chicago Press, 1980.

———. "Revolutions, Universals and Sexual Categories." *Salmagundi* 58–59 (Fall–Winter 1982–83): 89–113.

Brame, Gloria G., William D. Brame, and Jon Jacobs. *Different Loving: An Exploration of the World of Sexual Dominance and Submission.* London: Century, 1993.

Bravmann, Scott. *Queer Fictions of the Past: History, Culture, and Difference.* Cambridge: Cambridge University Press, 1997.

———. "*Stonewall,* Silver Screen: Cinematic Representation and the Queer Past." *American Quarterly* 48, no. 3 (Sept. 1996): 491–99.

Browning, Frank. *The Culture of Desire: Paradox and Perversity in Gay Lives Today.* New York: Crown, 1993.

Britzman, Deborah P. "On Becoming a 'Little Sex Researcher': Some Comments on a Polymorphously Perverse Curriculum." *Lost Subjects, Contested Objects: Toward a Psychoanalytic Inquiry of Learning.* Albany: State University of New York Press, 1998.

Burke, Phyllis. *Gender Shock: Exploding the Myths of Male and Female.* New York: Anchor/Doubleday, 1997.

Butler, Judith. "Doing Justice to Someone: Sex Reassignment and Allegories of Transsexuality." *GLQ: A Journal of Lesbian and Gay Studies* 7, no. 4 (2001): 621–36.

———. *Gender Trouble: Feminism and the Subversion of Identity.* New York: Routledge, 1990.

———. "Imitation and Gender Insubordination." In *Inside/Out: Lesbian Theories, Gay Theories,* edited by Diana Fuss, 13–31. New York: Routledge, 1991.

Califia, Pat[rick]. *Macho Sluts.* Los Angeles: Alyson, 1988.

———. *Public Sex: The Culture of Radical Sex.* Pittsburgh, Pa.: Cleis, 1994.

Cassels's Queer Companion: A Dictionary of Lesbian and Gay Life. Ed. William Stewart. London: Cassell, 1995.

Champagne, John. *The Blue Lady's Hands.* Secaucus, N.J.: Lyle Stuart, 1988.

———. *The Ethics of Marginality: A New Approach to Gay Studies.* Minneapolis: University of Minnesota Press, 1995.

Champagne, John, and Elayne Tobin. "'She's Right behind You': Gossip, Innuendo, and Rumor in the (De)Formation of Gay and Lesbian Studies." In *The Gay '90s: Disciplinary and Interdisciplinary Formations in Queer Studies,* edited by Thomas Foster, Carol Siegel, and Ellen E. Berry, 51–82. New York: New York University Press, 1997.

Clift, Eleanor. "How the Candidates Play to Gays." *Newsweek* 14 Sept. 1992, p. 40.

Clum, John M. "'And Once I Had It All': AIDS Narratives and Memories of an American Dream." In *Writing AIDS: Gay Literature, Language, and Analysis,* edited by Timothy F. Murphy and Suzanne Poirer, 200–224. New York: Columbia University Press, 1993.

———. "The Time before the War: AIDS, Memory, and Desire." *American Literature* 62, no. 4. (Dec. 1990): 648–67.

Commager, Henry Steele. *The American Mind.* New Haven, Conn.: Yale University Press, 1950.

Corbett, Ken. "Homosexual Boyhood: Notes on Girlyboys." In Rottnek, *Sissies and Tomboys,* 107–39.

Crimp, Douglas, ed. *AIDS: Cultural Analysis/Cultural Activism.* Cambridge, Mass.: MIT Press, 1988.

———. "AIDS: Cultural Analysis/Cultural Activism." In Crimp, *AIDS,* 3–16.

———. "How to Have Promiscuity in an Epidemic." In Crimp, *AIDS,* 237–71.

Cromwell, Jason. *Transmen and FTMs: Identities, Bodies, Gender, and Sexualities.* Urbana: University of Illinois Press, 1999.

D'Antonio, Michael. *The Fall from Grace: The Failed Crusade of the Christian Right.* New York: Farrar, 1989.

D'Emilio, John. Foreword to Jay and Young, *Out of the Closets,* xi–xxix.

———. *Making Trouble: Essays on Gay History, Politics, and the University.* New York: Routledge, 1992.

———. *Sexual Politics, Sexual Communities: The Making of a Homosexual Minority in the United States, 1940–1970.* Chicago: University of Chicago Press, 1983.

Denneny, Michael. "AIDS Writing and the Creation of a Gay Culture." In *Confronting AIDS through Literature,* edited by Judith Laurence Pastore, 36–54. Urbana: University of Illinois Press, 1993.

Diagnostic and Statistical Manual of Mental Disorders. 3d ed. Washington, D.C.: American Psychiatric Association, 1980.

Doty, Alexander. *Making Things Perfectly Queer: Interpreting Mass Culture.* Minneapolis: University of Minnesota Press, 1993.

Duberman, Martin. *Stonewall.* New York: Dutton, 1993.

Duggan, Lisa. "Making It Perfectly Queer." *Socialist Review* 92 (Jan.–Mar. 1992): 11–31. Repr. in Duggan and Hunter, *Sex Wars,* 155–72.

Duggan, Lisa, and Nan D. Hunter. *Sex Wars: Sexual Dissent and Political Culture.* New York: Routledge, 1995.

Easton, Dossie, and Catherine A. Liszt. *The Ethical Slut: A Guide to Infinite Sexual Possibilities.* San Francisco: Greenery, 1997.

Edwards, Blake, dir. *Victor/Victoria.* Film. Metro-Goldwyn-Mayer, 1982.

Elliott, Emory. "The Jeremiad." In *Cambridge History of American Literature,* 8 vols., edited by Sacvan Bercovitch, 1:255–78. Cambridge: Cambridge University Press, 1994.

Escoffier, Jeffrey. "Inside the Ivory Closet: The Challenge Facing Gay and Lesbian Studies." *American Homo: Community and Perversity,* 104–17. Berkeley: University of California Press, 1998.

Feinberg, David B. *Eighty-Sixed.* New York: Viking, 1989.

Feinberg, Leslie. *Stone Butch Blues: A Novel.* Ithaca, N.Y.: Firebrand, 1993.

Finch, Nigel, dir. *Stonewall.* Videocassette. BMG Home Video, 1998 [1995].

FitzGerald, Frances. *Cities on a Hill: A Journey through Contemporary American Cultures.* New York: Touchstone, 1987.

Fitzgerald, F. Scott. "The Crack-Up." *The Crack-Up with Other Pieces and Stories.* Harmondsworth, U.K.: Penguin, 1979.

Foucault, Michel. *The Archeology of Knowledge.* Trans. A. M. Sheridan Smith. New York: Pantheon Books, 1972.

———. "The End of the Monarchy of Sex." Trans. Dudley M. Marchi. In *Foucault Live: Interviews, 1966–84,* edited by Sylvère Lotringer, 137–55. New York: Semiotext(e), 1989.

———. "The Ethic of Care for the Self as a Practice of Freedom." Interview. By Raul Fornet-Betancourt, Helmut Becker, and Alfredo Gomez-Müller. Trans. J. D. Gauthier. In *The Final Foucault,* 1–20.

———. *Ethics: Subjectivity and Truth.* Vol. 1 of *The Essential Works of Michel Foucault, 1954–1984.* Ed. Paul Rabinow. New York: Free Press, 1997.

———. *The Final Foucault.* Ed. James Bernauer and David Rasmussen. Cambridge, Mass.: MIT Press, 1988.

———. "Friendship as a Way of Life." Interview. By R. de Ceccaty, J. Danet, and J. Le Bitoux. Trans. John Johnston. In Foucault, *Ethics,* 135–40.

———. *The History of Sexuality,* vol. 2: *The Use of Pleasure.* Trans. Robert Hurley. New York: Vintage Books, 1986.

———. *The History of Sexuality,* vol. 3: *The Care of the Self.* Trans. Robert Hurley. New York: Vintage Books, 1988.

———. "Sex, Power and the Politics of Identity." Interview. By Bob Gallagher and Alexander Wilson. *The Advocate,* 7 August 1984, pp. 26–30, 58.

———. "Sexual Choice, Sexual Act." Interview. By James O'Higgins. *Salmagundi* 58–59 (Fall 1982–Winter 1983): 10–24.

———. "Technologies of the Self." In Foucault, *Ethics,* 223–51.

"Frank Urges Gays to Avoid Extremes." *Wisconsin Light,* 28 Apr.–11 May 1994, p. 2.

Fuss, Diana. *Essentially Speaking: Feminism, Nature, and Difference.* New York: Routledge, 1989.

Gallop, Jane. *Around 1981: Academic Feminist Literary Theory.* New York: Routledge, 1992.

Goldman, Ruth. "Who Is That *Queer* Queer? Exploring Norms around Sexuality, Race, and Class in Queer Theory." In Beemyn and Eliason, *Queer Studies,* 169–82.

Goldstein, Lynda. "Queer Theory: The Monster That Is Destroying Lesbianville." In Mintz and Rothblum, *Lesbians in Academia,* 261–68.

Green, Richard. "Gender Identity Disorder in Children." In *Treatments of Psychiatric Disorders,* 2d ed., 2 vols., edited by Glen O. Gabbard, 2:2001–14. Washington, D.C.: American Psychiatric Press, 1995.

———. The *"Sissy Boy Syndrome" and the Development of Homosexuality.* New Haven, Conn.: Yale University Press, 1987.

Greyson, John, dir. *The ADS Epidemic.* Videocassette. Frameline, 1987.

Halberstam, Judith. "On Location: Drag Kings in London, San Francisco, and New York." In Halberstam and Volcano, *Drag King Book,* 64–109.

———. *Female Masculinity.* Durham, N.C.: Duke University Press, 1998.

Halberstam, Judith, and Del LaGrace Volcano. *The Drag King Book.* London: Serpent's Tail, 1999.

Hale, C. Jacob. "Leatherdyke Boys and Their Daddies: How to Have Sex without Women or Men." *Social Text* 52–53 (1997): 223–36.

Halperin, David. *Saint Foucault: Towards a Gay Hagiography.* New York: Oxford University Press, 1995.

Haraway, Donna. "A Cyborg Manifesto: Science, Technology, and Socialist-Feminism in the Late Twentieth Century." *Simians, Cyborgs, and Women: The Reinvention of Nature,* 149–81. New York: Routledge, 1991.

Hart, Lynda. *Between the Body and the Flesh: Performing Sadomasochism.* New York: Columbia University Press, 1998.

Himmelfarb, Gertrude. "Some Reflections on the New History." *American Historical Review* 94, no. 3 (June 1989): 661–70.

Hofstadter, Richard. *The American Political Tradition and the Men Who Made It.* New York: Knopf, 1948.

Hogan, Christopher. Review of *Stonewall,* dir. Nigel Finch. *Cineaste* 22, no. 3 (Dec. 1996): 36–38.

Hughes, Holly. *Clit Notes: A Sapphic Sampler.* New York: Grove, 1996.

Jagose, Annamarie. *Queer Theory: An Introduction.* New York: New York University Press, 1996.

Jay, Karla, and Allen Young, eds. *Out of the Closets: Voices of Gay Liberation.* New York: New York University Press, 1992 [1972].

Jeffreys, Sheila. "The Queer Disappearance of Lesbians." In Mintz and Rothblum, *Lesbians in Academia,* 269–78.

Johnston, Jill. "Firestorm on Christopher Street." In Fred W. McDarrah and Timothy

S. McDarrah, *Gay Pride: Photographs from Stonewall to Today,* ix–xi. Chicago: A Capella, 1994.

Kakutani, Michiko. "In Fiction, AIDS Finds New Forms." *New York Times,* 12 March 1993, pp. B1, B8.

Katz, Jonathan. *Gay American History: Lesbians and Gay Men in the U.S.A.* New York: Avon Books, 1978.

Keller, James R. *Queer (Un) Friendly Film and Television.* Jefferson, N.C.: McFarland, 2002.

Kramer, Larry. *Reports from the Holocaust: The Making of an AIDS Activist.* New York: St Martin's, 1989.

Kuhn, Annette. *The Power of the Image: Essays on Representation and Sexuality.* London: Routledge, 1985.

LaCapra, Dominick. *History and Criticism.* Ithaca, N.Y.: Cornell University Press, 1985.

Levine, Martin P. *Gay Macho: The Life and Death of the Homosexual Clone.* New York: New York University Press, 1998.

Macey, David. *The Lives of Michel Foucault: A Biography.* New York: Pantheon, 1993.

Malinowitz, Harriet. "Lesbian Studies and Postmodern Queer Theory." In *The New Lesbian Studies: Into the Twenty-First Century,* edited by Bonnie Zimmerman and Toni A. H. McNaron. New York: Feminist Press, 1996.

Marcus, Eric. *Making Gay History: The Half-Century Fight for Lesbian and Gay Equal Rights.* New York: Perennial/HarperCollins, 2002.

———. *Making History: The Struggle for Gay and Lesbian Equal Rights, 1945–1990.* New York: Perennial/HarperCollins, 1993.

McCann, Richard. "My Mother's Clothes: The School of Beauty and Shame." In *Men on Men 2: Best New Gay Fiction,* edited by George Stambolian, 13–31. New York: New American Library, 1988.

Midler, Bette. *Mud Will Be Flung Tonight!* Atlantic Records 81291–2.

Mintner, Shannon. "Diagnosis and Treatment of Gender Identity Disorder in Children." In Rottnek, *Sissies and Tomboys,* 9–33.

Mintz, Beth, and Esther Rothblum, eds. *Lesbians in Academia: Degrees of Freedom.* New York: Routledge, 1997.

Monette, Paul. *Afterlife.* New York: Crown, 1990.

———. *Borrowed Time: An AIDS Memoir.* New York: Harcourt, 1988.

Moore, Oscar. *A Matter of Life and Sex.* New York: Dutton, 1992.

Morris, Meaghan. "in any event . . ." In *Men in Feminism,* edited by Alice Jardine and Paul Smith, 173–81. New York: Methuen, 1987.

Moser, Charles, and J. J. Madeson. *Bound to Be Free: The SM Experience.* New York: Continuum, 1999.

Munson, Marcia, and Judith P. Stelboum, eds. *The Lesbian Polyamory Reader: Open*

Relationships, Non-Monogamy, and Casual Sex. New York: Harrington Park, 1999.

Nestle, Joan. "My History with Censorship." In *A Restricted Country,* 144–50. Ithaca, N.Y.: Firebrand, 1987.

Nicolosi, Joseph. *Reparative Therapy of Male Homosexuality: A New Clinical Approach.* Northvale, N.J.: Jason Aronson, 1991.

Peirce, Kimberly, dir. *Boys Don't Cry.* Film. Twnetieth Century Fox, 1999.

Pela, Robert L. "Stonewall's Eyewitnesses." *The Advocate* 3 May 1994, pp. 50–55.

Piontek, Thomas. "John Champagne." In *Contemporary Gay American Novelists: A Bio-Bibliographical Critical Sourcebook,* edited by Emmanuel S. Nelson, 65–70. Westport, Conn.: Greenwood, 1993.

———. "Kinging in the Heartland; or, The Power of Marginality." *Journal of Homosexuality* 43, nos. 3–4 (2002): 125–43.

———. "Unsafe Representations: Cultural Criticism in the Age of AIDS." In Piontek and Kader, *Essays,* 128–53.

Piontek, Thomas, and Cheryl Kader, eds. *Essays in Gay and Lesbian Studies.* Special issue. *Discourse* 15, no. 1 (Fall–Winter 1992).

Popular Memory Group. "Popular Memory: Theory, Politics, Method." In *Making Histories: Studies in History Writing and Politics,* edited by Richard Johnson, Gregor McLennan, Bill Schwarz, and David Sutton, 205–52. Minneapolis: University of Minnesota Press, 1982.

Poster, Mark. Introduction to Baudrillard, *Selected Writings,* 1–9.

Praunheim, Rosa von [Holger Mischwitzky], dir. *Nicht der Homosexuelle ist pervers, sondern die Situation, in der er lebt.* Film. 1970.

Queen, Carol A. "The Leather Daddy and the Femme." In *Doing It for Daddy,* edited by Pat Califia, 24–32, 152–61. Los Angeles: Alyson, 1994.

———. *The Leather Daddy and the Femme: An Erotic Novel in Several Scenes and a Few Conversations.* San Francisco, Calif.: Down There, 2003.

Reese, Laura. *Topping from Below.* New York: St. Martin's, 1995.

Reich, June. "Genderfuck: The Law of the Dildo." In Piontek and Kader, *Essays,* 112–27.

Rekers, George. "Inadequate Sex Role Differentiation in Childhood: The Family and Gender Identity Disorders." *Journal of Family and Culture* 2, no. 7 (1987): 8–37.

Rotello, Gabriel. *Sexual Ecology: AIDS and the Destiny of Gay Men.* New York: Dutton, 1997.

Rottnek, Matthew, ed. *Sissies and Tomboys: Gender Nonconformity and Homosexual Childhood.* New York: New York University Press, 1999.

Rubin, Gayle. "Thinking Sex: Notes for a Radical Theory of the Politics of Sex." In Vance, *Pleasure and Danger,* 267–319.

———. "The Catacombs: A Temple to the Butthole." In *Leatherfolk: Radical Sex,*

People, Politics, and Practice, edited by Mark Thompson, 119–41. Boston: Alyson, 1991.

———. "Of Catamites and Kings: Reflections on Butch, Gender, and Boundaries." In *The Persistent Desire: A Femme-Butch Reader,* edited by Joan Nestle, 466–83. Boston: Alyson, 1992.

Said, Edward. *Beginnings: Intention and Method.* New York: Basic Books, 1975.

Schiller, Greta, dir. *Before Stonewall: The Making of a Gay and Lesbian Community.* Videocassette. MPI Home Video, 1989.

Scott, Joan Wallach. "History in Crisis? The Others' Side of the Story." *American Historical Review* 94, no. 3 (June 1989): 680–92.

Sedgwick, Eve Kosofsky. *Epistemology of the Closet.* Berkeley: University of California Press, 1990.

———. "How to Bring Your Kids Up Gay: The War on Effeminate Boys." In Kosofsky, *Tendencies,* 154–64. Durham, N.C.: Duke University Press, 1993.

Seidman, Steven. *Embattled Eros: Sexual Politics and Ethics in Contemporary America.* New York: Routledge, 1992.

———. "Symposium: Queer Theory/Sociology: A Dialogue." *Sociological Theory* 12, no. 2 (1994): 166–77.

Signorile, Michelangelo. *Life Outside: The Signorile Report on Gay Men: Sex, Drugs, Muscles, and the Passages of Life.* New York: HarperCollins, 1997.

Smith, Barbara. "Queer Politics: Where's the Revolution?" *The Nation,* 5 July 1993, pp. 12–15.

Smyth, Cherry. *Lesbians Talk Queer Notions.* London: Scarlett, 1992.

Snitow, Ann, Christine Stansell, and Sharon Thompson, eds. *Powers of Desire: The Politics of Sexuality.* New York: Monthly Review Press, 1983.

Straayer, Chris. "Redressing the 'Natural': The Temporary Transvestite Film." *Wide Angle* 14, no. 1 (1992): 36–55.

Sullivan, Andrew. *Virtually Normal: An Argument about Homosexuality.* New York: Knopf, 1995.

Sullivan, Nikki. *A Critical Introduction to Queer Theory.* New York: New York University Press, 2003.

Teal, Donn. *The Gay Militants.* New York: Stein and Day, 1971.

"'Thinking Sex/Thinking Gender': The GLQ Forum." Intro. by Annamarie Jagose and Don Kulick. *GLQ: A Journal of Lesbian and Gay Studies* 10, no. 2 (2004): 211–312.

Thomas, Kevin. Review of *Stonewall,* dir. Nigel Finch. *Los Angeles Times,* 26 July 1996, p. 12.

Timmons, Stuart. *The Trouble with Harry Hay: Founder of the Modern Gay Movement.* Boston: Alyson, 1990.

Tucker, Scott. "Well, Was It Worth It?" In *Personal Dispatches: Writers Confront AIDS,* edited by John Preston, 124–32. New York: St. Martin's, 1989.

Turque, Bill. "Gays under Fire." *Newsweek,* 14 Sept. 1992, pp. 35–40.

Vance, Carole S., ed. *Pleasure and Danger: Exploring Female Sexuality.* New York: Routledge, 1984.

Warner, Michael. Introduction to *Fear of a Queer Planet: Queer Politics and Social Theory,* edited by Michael Warner, vii–xxi. Minneapolis: University of Minnesota Press, 1993.

———. *The Trouble with Normal: Sex, Politics, and the Ethics of Queer Life.* New York: Free Press, 1999.

Weiss, Andrea. *Before Stonewall: An Illustrated Guide to the Emmy Award Winning Film.* Tallahassee, Fla.: Naiad, 1988.

West, Celeste. *Lesbian Polyfidelity: A Pleasure Guide for All Women Whose Hearts Are Open to Multiple Sensualoves, or, How to Keep Nonmonogamy Safe, Sane, Honest and Laughing, You Rogue!* San Francisco: Booklegger, 1996.

White, Hayden. "The Burden of History." *Tropics of Discourse: Essays in Cultural Criticism,* 27–50. Baltimore, Md.: Johns Hopkins University Press, 1978.

———. *Metahistory: The Historical Imagination in Nineteenth-Century Europe.* Baltimore, Md.: Johns Hopkins University Press, 1973.

Wilchins, Riki Anne. *Read My Lips: Sexual Subversion and the End of Gender.* Ithaca, N.Y.: Firebrand Books, 1997.

———. "Time for Gender Rights." *GLQ: A Journal of Lesbian and Gay Studies* 10, no. 2 (2004): 265–67.

Yingling, Thomas E. "Sexual Preference/Cultural Reference: The Predicament of Gay Culture Studies." *American Literary History* 3, no. 1 (Spring 1991): 184–97.

Young, Allen. "Out of the Closets, Into the Streets." In Jay and Young, *Out of the Closets,* 6–31.

Index

THOMAS PIONTEK is a visiting assistant professor of English at Otterbein College in Westerville, Ohio. His areas of specialization include gender and sexuality studies, queer theory, film, cultural studies, and American literature.

The University of Illinois Press
is a founding member of the
Association of American University Presses.

———————————————————————

Composed in 10.5/13 Minion
with Meta display
at the University of Illinois Press
Manufactured by Sheridan Books, Inc.

University of Illinois Press
1325 South Oak Street
Champaign, IL 61820-6903
www.press.uillinois.edu